Antisocial Commentary

from the secret files of the
Mattress Police

Antisocial Commentary: From the Secret Files of the Mattress Police

Copyright ©2007 by Rob Kroese

All rights reserved. No portion of this book may be reproduced, stored in a retrieval system, or transmitted in any form or by any means – electronic, mechanical, photocopy, recording or other – except for brief quotations in reviews, without the prior permission of the author.

Published by Mattress Police Books in conjunction with Lulu Press.

"Rustic Motel" picture on page 63 is copyright of Jody Miller (http://flickr.com/photos/jodymiller/)

Moon photo on page 126 is courtesy of http://www.freeimages.co.uk/.

Lyrics to "Sexy Back," "Every Time We Touch," and "You're Beautiful" are copyrighted by their respective owners.

The Incredible Hulk is a registered trademark of Marvel Comics.

Batman, Robin, Superman and Wonder-Woman are registered trademarks of DC Comics.

Star Wars, Boba Fett, Jabba the Hutt, Death Star, Star Destroyer and other Star Wars creations and characters are registered trademarks of LucasFilm Ltd.

Frisbee is a registered trademark of Wham-O, Inc.

Harry Potter is a registered trademark of Warner Bros.

ISBN 978-0-6151-5484-8

Visit **www.mattresspolice.com**
for more semi-coherent drivel!

Tagus Intactus

Civitatus Intactus

(The Sacred Seal of the Fraternal Order of Mattress Police)

www.mattresspolice.com

Preface	5
Introduction	7
A Note on Coarse Language	11
1. Enough About Me (for Now)	**13**
Thee Eagle Has Landed	14
The Dawning of the Age of Diesel	16
The Butt of My Own Joke	19
Valdyrre, I Hardly Knew Ye	21
How to Write a Funny Blog	22
A Cautionary Message for the Class of 2007	24
A Fitting Tribute	26
The Lark Never Expected to Become Famous Just for Being a Silly Bird Either	29
Even a Traffic Whore Has Some Standards	30
Construction and Deconstruction	33
Review: The Widow of Turmeric Falls	36
2. The Family	**39**
Happy Inappropriate Card Day!	42
The Straight, the Narrow and the Raunchy	43
La-Z-Girl	47
As Easy as One, Two	50
Bills and Other Pests	51
Ripon Man Discovers New Dinosaur Species	52
Dumber than a Post	55
"Are You the Responsible Parent?"	59
Aloha! And Good Riddance!	61
3. Driving	**65**
WTF?	66
State of Anxiety	69
Failure to Appear	70
Just Give Me a Sign	75
The California Driver Test	76
Perpetual Motion	81
Don't Try This When Not at Home	84
4. Culture, Pop and Otherwise	**85**
The Force is Middling in this One	86
Harry Potter and the Inevitable Slide into Satanism	90
Reality Bites	92
Congratulations on Your New Testicles!	94
The Best Things in Life Are Free (Unless You Are Stupid)	96

Don't Make Me Angry	98
A Conversation Overheard in the Batcave	100
Superman Returns: The Unreleased Version	102
Brilliant! (James Blunt's Songwriting Journal)	106
Bringing Snarky Back	109

5. Politics and Current Events — **111**

Fed Chair Speaks Out Against Smiley Inflation	112
World's Worst Dictator	115
Can't We All Just Get Along?	116
2020 Vision	119
Talk Like a Man	121
Harvard to Settle Question of God's Existence	123
Bush Fiddles While Moon Deteriorates	125
A Crude Proposal	129
Undocumented Thoughts	131
May the Force Be with Me	133
Belgium: France Keeps Touching Me	136

6. Fiction and Unabashed Hyperbole — **137**

I Do Mind! I Do!	138
Mixed Fruits and Metaphors	140
A Slurry of Monsters	145
What I Learned This Morning from a Sea Turtle	148
Imagine My Surprise	149
How the Almond Farmer Saved Christmas	151
The Legend of Diesel	155

Preface

*In which the reader's giddy hopes are immediately
dashed like so many miniature porcelain geese.*

This book is not about mattresses. Nor is it about police.

I know, the title is misleading. You probably expected it to be about the mythical mattress police who throw you in jail for removing the tags from your mattresses. Boy, wouldn't that be funny? 160 pages of mattress police jokes. It would be like watching one of those interminable movies based on a *Saturday Night Live* sketch.

No, I'm afraid there's no good explanation for this book's title, except for the fact that most of the material herein was previously published on my website, MattressPolice.com. MattressPolice.com got its name the way that everything on the Internet gets its name: Somebody punches names into a search engine until they find one that's available. These days it's just about impossible to find a decent name that hasn't already been taken, which is why everything on the Internet is named Zazzzooomm or Slakr or something. I suppose having spent more hours during college watching *Fletch* than studying probably had something to do with it too.

The next question on your mind (besides "Why would I buy this book if I can read most of this stuff for free on your website?") is probably, "Diesel? What the hell kind of stupid name is 'Diesel'?"

I honestly have no good answer for that either. I just always thought Diesel was a cool name. Yes, even before Vin Diesel graced us with his thespian antics and terrific deltoids. It's just such a blunt, forceful, manly name. So much so, in fact, that nobody ever thought to call me it.

A few years ago I started working for a company where there was already somebody named Rob. You know how every other kid today is named Dylan, Austin or Tyler? Forty years ago all of those kids would have been named Rob. So I'm used to running into Robs, Bobs and Roberts everywhere I go, but this was a special case because it so happened that this other Rob was a world-class wanker.

Being really only a bush league wanker myself, I wanted to be sure not to be confused with this other Rob. For a while I introduced myself as "not the bad Rob." I would add, by way of clarification, that there wasn't necessarily a bad Rob, but if there was one, I wasn't him. This constant explication grew tiresome for me and, presumably, for the other Rob. Someone made the mistake of asking me if I'd prefer to be called by a nickname.

I said, without even having to think about it, "I want to be called *Diesel*."

And to my surprise, the name stuck. I think it started out ironic, like with short guys who get called Stretch, but after a while everybody just called me Diesel, as if that's what my Mama had put on my birth certificate. When I started blogging, there was no question regarding what pseudonym I would use.

So that's the non-explanation for why this book is called what it is and why I'm called what I am. Now was there another question pending? Oh yeah, that thing about why you should buy this book. Well, for one thing there's this preface that explains everything so nicely. And don't look now, but I think there's an introduction coming up!

Introduction

During which the reader wonders how it's possible that this book rates both a preface and an introduction.

This book started with a sea turtle.

More precisely, it started when someone I worked with coaxed me into setting up a MySpace page. For those of you who aren't tech-savvy, MySpace is an "online community" that combines all the worst aspects of the Internet into one difficult-to-use and horrifically ugly package. Bad web design; applications that don't work properly; self-absorbed teenagers communicating in a barely coherent mélange of abbreviations, emoticons and pop-culture clichés; an endless barrage of desperate singles ads; sexual predators looking for the aforementioned teenagers: MySpace has it all.

This was in 2006, just after MySpace was bought for 80 gazillion dollars by Rupert Murdoch, who was hoping to make Fox News look respectable by comparison. I had been working as a professional web developer for nearly ten years at that point, so one would assume that I would have possessed the requisite technical background to set up a MySpace account.

One would be wrong.

My first attempts to set up a MySpace failed, presumably because the MySpace robot could sense my lack of familiarity with Christina Aguilera and *The Suite Life of Zach and Cody*. It's as if the site is designed to be understood only by teenagers (and, of course, fifty year old men who have a lot of practice thinking like teenagers).

Once I had gotten a 23 year old coworker to set up my account, I was in business. I set about uploading pictures of myself, listing my favorite movies and TV shows and picking a profile song.... and then I remembered I wasn't a fourteen year old girl. Why was I doing this? Who was I trying to impress by listing Def Leppard and Audioslave as two of my favorite bands?

I started over, selecting movies (*Steel Magnolias*, *Iron Eagle*, *Mercury Rising*) purely for their metallurgical properties. I listed my interests as moping, procrastinating, and shirking. I cited Batman, Wolverine and Immanuel Kant as my heroes. And then I started to write my first blog post.

In my experience most blogs are made up of stultifyingly dull anecdotes of daily life told as if they were unbelievably exciting. Whoever said "Write what you know" deserves a fair amount of blame for the eight hundred billion blog posts on the Internet about poopy diapers and newborn kittens. In "How to Write a Funny Blog" (Chapter 1) I coined the term *manicdote* for "stories that have a sense of urgency but otherwise are of absolutely no interest to anyone."

I decided to write the opposite of a manicdote, relating a fantastically bizarre (and entirely made-up) incident in a completely low-key, unemotive manner. I wrote it in about two minutes, without stopping to think what it was about or whether it even made any sense. The result was a short, strange piece of fiction called "What I Learned This Morning from a Sea Turtle" (Chapter 6). I suppose I was unconsciously emulating the inemulatable Douglas Adams. It begins:

> "I was accosted this morning by a large sea turtle. I had arisen early to steal the neighbor's newspaper (I cancelled my subscription when I learned the editor was a freethinker and a bigamist), and just as I stepped outside, I saw it. The turtle must have been a good 5 feet long and 3.5 feet wide (these are shell measurements), and I would estimate that it weighed at least 200 pounds. I certainly couldn't lift him, and I'm hella strong. I attribute my exceptional strength to a daily regimen of vitamins and backgammon, although I'm also 1/32 Apache Indian, so that's sort of an X factor."

The story continues in that vein for a few more paragraphs before climaxing in an orgy of incoherence. I had so much fun with it that I went on to write a review of a nonexistent movie. I introduced it thusly:

> "I've always wanted to make a movie. I've also kind of always wanted to be a big-time movie critic. As neither of those dreams is likely to come true, I've decided to simply write a review of the movie that I would have made if I weren't such a loser. Here it is."

And I proceeded to mercilessly pan my own imaginary movie:

"The camera work is amateurish, alternating inexplicably between a jittery hand held camera and a slightly less jittery camera attached to a long bamboo pole. The latter third of the film is essentially a PowerPoint Presentation, which drains the climax of much of its dramatic impact."

(The full review of *The Widow of Turmeric Falls* appears in Chapter 1).

I emailed the link to my blog to a few friends, who encouraged me to keep writing. Eventually I abandoned MySpace and moved to my own web site, MattressPolice.com. I tried to maintain the level of absurdity I had achieved in my first two posts, but absurdity can't exist in a vacuum; it's only absurd against a backdrop of normalcy. So more and more of my real life crept into my blog. Still, I like to think that one of the nice things about MattressPolice.com is that you never know what to expect on a given day. Frankly, I don't always know what to expect. I often start writing about one thing, go off on a tangent, and never get back to what it was I meant to say.

One of the consequences of this "method" is that I have no room for an agenda. I have religious and political convictions to be sure (and these occasionally come out in my writing), but for me the kiss of death for a humor piece is to start off trying to convince someone of a particular point of view. I believe in the power of humor. I don't mean that humor is an effective way of making a point; I mean that humor *is* the point. To me, if something is funny, it must have some element of truth. Humor is making connections between seemingly unrelated things; seeing something that you never noticed before even though it was there all along.

MattressPolice.com started out as – and will always remain – an experiment. I've tried out every type of humor writing I could think of, from satirical news stories to simple observational humor to borderline gibberish. An essential part of that experiment is my readers, who have provided invaluable encouragement and feedback via blog comments and emails. I've never subscribed to the idea that writing is a solitary activity – in "Promote Your Blog" (which appears in Chapter 3), I facetiously suggest that bloggers shouldn't allow readers to post comments on their blogs: "Real writers don't need endless validation from their readers…. If you do allow comments for some reason, for the love of Moses don't respond to them. That erodes the holy wall of separation between blogger and reader."

Sadly, there seem to be a lot of bloggers who subscribe to this view. Personally, I'm convinced that I'd have given up long ago if it weren't for the encouragement and constructive criticism of my loyal readers. I've said before, without a hint of sarcasm, that I've got the best damn readership in the blogosphere, and I challenge anyone to dispute that.

So this is for you guys – my fellow bloggers as well as the commenters, and even the faceless lurkers who keep anonymously pushing up my traffic stats. Thanks, everybody, and enjoy!

A Note on Coarse Language
(and Other Things that May Rub One the Wrong Way)

In which the author covers his ass.

I try to avoid profanity and crude humor, but sometimes there's just no satisfactory synonym for *asshole*. *Shit* is sprinkled throughout this book, and you'll run into the occasional *dumbass*. I've drawn the line at the f-word, however. Three lines, actually, which is why you'll see a few instances of *f---*. You're welcome to fill in the spaces with any letters, numbers or symbols for has-been pop stars that you like.

I've never really understood why certain words are considered *verboten*. We frown on *shit*, shrug our shoulders at *crap*, and smile approvingly at *excrement*. Generally the more blunt and Anglo-Saxon-sounding the word is, the more likely it is to be offensive. The longer and more French-sounding the word is, the more likely it is to be acceptable. *Snot* is hard to swallow, but *phlegm* goes down no problem. Well you know what? F--- the French. There is a reason that Monty Python is British and Jerry Lewis is French. The French are so busy trying to look impressive and sound good that they wouldn't know a funny word if it bit them on their collective *derriere*.

The only sensible moral restriction on language that I know of is the Third Commandment (Second if you're Catholic or Lutheran): "Don't misuse the name of God." That makes sense to me. I don't even like it when my wife yells my name across the house because there's a spider or something. Imagine how God feels with 6 billion people calling upon His name every time they stub their little toe. (Come to think of it, God, you *do* have some explaining to do regarding that little toe. What is that, some kind of joke? I mean, You had to know we were going to invent coffee tables eventually, right?) So I try to avoiding taking the Lord's name in vain, except in some of my fiction, where a character may occasionally curse. In the same way, while I try to avoid biting people's faces off in real life, my characters may not feel the same compunction.

Despite my efforts to limit my use of the Devil's language, there is a particular group of people who might take offense at some passages in this book. These are the people who take themselves way too seriously. So let's go over this once, just so we're on the same page: These are *jokes*, people. If you find something in this book particularly offensive to your sensibilities, assume that it's sarcasm. That way your sensibilities will remain intact, and you will have a new appreciation for my wry sense of irony. It's win-win.

Yes, I make fun of fundamentalists. No, that doesn't mean that I hate Christians. It means that I think God expects a little more from us than to let other people do our thinking for us.

Yes, I make jokes about homosexuality. No, that doesn't mean I'm homophobic, any more than making jokes about spiders makes me arachnophobic. It also doesn't make me a spider, in case you're wondering.

I could go on, but I'm bored, and you get the idea. If it makes you feel better, you can burn this book when you're done. We'll make more.

1

Enough About Me (for Now)

*At which point the reader is oddly reassured
to find him- or herself in the land of numbered chapters.*

In putting together material for this book, I've noticed that a lot of my essays are centered on a common theme: me.

I'm obsessed with myself in a way that few other people are. If I was any more interested in every little detail of my life, I'd be ordered by a judge to stay a hundred yards away from myself at all times. Which, of course, would make it very difficult for me to maintain proper oral hygiene.

Many of my essays are thinly veiled attempts to communicate to the world just how great I am. Even more of them are completely unveiled, and sometimes these posts are so over-the-top that any sane person would assume that I'm being facetious. I suppose I am, but presumably there is something a little wrong with someone who writes, even facetiously, so often on the topic of himself. I mean, it would be

Another of my adoring fans.

one thing if I had cured cancer or if I had the longest peacetime expansion in U.S. history under my belt (if you get my drift). I have no good reason to write so much about myself, but I do. In fact, I'm doing it right now. Of course, I'm writing about what a jerk I am, but that's a form of self-deprecation, which I'm told people find charming. The only thing better than getting to be a jerk is telling people what a jerk I am and having people nod approvingly and say, "And so modest!"

Anyway, if you've had enough of me blathering about myself, you might want to skip this chapter and dive right into chapter 4, which is the funniest one. After that, you'll have been fully schooled in my brilliance and you can return to this chapter with a renewed tolerance for my narcissism.

Ready? Here's to me!

Thee Eagle Has Landed

I wrote my first novel in second grade.

Well, maybe more of a novella. It was 50 pages long. Although come to think of it, part of it was written on little kids' paper, so maybe it was more like 20 big people pages. You know the stuff that I'm talking about. The paper that's somewhere in between grocery bag material and industrial paper towel in terms of texture, so that occasionally your O's would look like Q's because your pencil had to jump over a chunk of wood pulp. It had like eight extra lines on it of all different colors so that you could see how bad your penmanship was.

"Diesel, the top of the loop of your 'd' should be on the red line."

"What 'd'? I don't see any 'd'."

"Right here. In the word 'ditch.'"

"Nope, don't see it."

"Here! Right here, plain as day!"

"Well if it's plain as day, why are you making such a big deal out of it?"

"Diesel!"

"I think I might have that dyspepsi thing you were talking about."

"Why?"

"That's not a 'd'. I'm writing a story about you."

Actually my 2nd grade teacher was really nice. Also, she loved me. Early in the year she instructed the class to write a story, and I wrote one about Captain Bill and his spaceship Thee Eagle. No, not *The* Eagle. *Thee* Eagle, is in, "Hey, is that *Thee* Eagle?" And it was. Although my teacher later renamed Thee Eagle to Thee Eagle With A Line Through the Second 'e,' for reasons that were unclear to me. I guess she just wanted Captain Bill's spaceship to have a more unique name, in case it ever needed to race Seabiscuit.

Captain Bill and his crew had all kinds of adventures in their big black ship that resembled a partially peeled and very overripe banana. I recall that they went to Jupiter, but I'm not sure why. Then again, why does anyone go to Jupiter? It's the strip clubs and legalized cockfights, am I right? What happens on Jupiter stays on Jupiter. Mostly because of the crushing gravity.

The story of Captain Bill and Thee Eagle never ended, for the simple reason that once I finished the story I would have to do insufferably dull things like add 3 and 7. I didn't understand why they needed *me* to do this. I was like, "It's 1977, people! Arabic numerals have been around for 1400 years and nobody has figured out 3 plus 7 yet? Don't you people have scientists for this sort of work?" I mean, hell, we even had calculators back in 1977. I used to cart mine around in a radio flyer. But no, they insisted that we do this drudge work by hand. And not only that, but after a while I realized we were doing *the same problems over and over.* "Who is keeping records at this place?" I demanded. "I swear I just multiplied 3 by 4 yesterday! Oh, that was 4 times 3. Never mind. Man, I wish somebody would discover the commutative property of multiplication."

"So... do I need to do math now?" I would ask Mrs. P.

"Oh, you just keep working on your story," she said.

No freaking way! I thought. *Mrs. P. is the coolest teacher ever!* After that, Mrs. P. started making appearances in the story. Captain Bill and she once took some unauthorized leave on Jupiter, if you get my meaning.

In this fashion, the saga of Captain Bill and Thee Eagle went on, and on, and on, page after page after page until I ran out of grocery bag paper and moved on to the real stuff. It must have been the longest story ever written by a second grader. I never did end it. Eventually I think I lost the manuscript (I was forever losing things as a child), and had to move on. But in some ways the story still lives on. Sometimes when I'm weighed down by the drudgery of life, I imagine Captain Bill swooping down in Thee Eagle to save the day.

"Thank goodness you're here, Captain Bill! I'm a church treasurer now and I could really use your help. What's 3 plus 7?"

And Captain Bill would just shrug and say, "Dunno. Let's get wasted and go to Jupiter. I left Mrs. P. frozen in carbonite, so she looks the same as she did in 1977."

"Sweeet," I'd say, with an extra 'e' just for the hell of it.

The Dawning of the Age of Diesel

I am now 37 years old. In many cultures, 37 is considered quite old. If I had lived in ancient Greece, for example, I'd be dead by now. Sobering thought, isn't it?

Reaching this milestone has prompted me to reflect upon my life. I've had many good years, a few bad years, and several pretty decent 20 minute interludes on Sunday afternoons while the kids were watching the Cartoon Network. So far, the naughties (that's what I'm calling the current decade; I'm hoping it will start to catch on in the next year or two) have been a good decade for me. I built a house and had a daughter, and both of them continue to get bigger; it remains to be seen which of them I will have to sell to afford the other.

In the nineties I graduated from college, got married, got my first "real" job, had a son and bought a house. Hmmm, what was the downside of the 90s for me again? Oh yeah, crippling depression! The panic attacks, the crying jags.... good times.

The seventies and eighties were ok overall, but I think my favorite decade was the sixties. Those of you who lived through the sixties know what I'm talking about. It was such a peaceful, relaxing time. I swear, I did nothing for the first nine years of the sixties. I mean, I'm talking *nothing*. If people asked, I would tell them I was experimenting with the Heideggerian notion of non-being, but in truth I was mostly just chillin'.

I have Woodstock to thank for my conception. My dad walked up to my mom, who was sitting on a blanket in the sun with flowers in her hair, and said, "Hey, are you done with that newspaper? I haven't read today's *Peanuts*. I love Snoopy's little bird friend." Well, it turned out that my mom hadn't read it either, so there they sat, taking their break on a dumpster behind DOW chemical's Agent Orange plant, reading *Peanuts* together. My mom took the vowels and my dad took the consonants, and just like that, it was love. Which was a good thing, because they had been married for six years.

As they laughed over Snoopy's unnatural exploits with his avian companion, my future parents la la la la la la la I can't hear you I have my hands over my ears la la la la la la la la la can't hear anything la la la la la la la la la la think about something else la la la la la la la la la la la la la la la pi to the 16th digit is is 3.141592653589793 la la la la la la la la la la la la la la la and just like that I was conceived.

That's when things started to really happen for me. Probably the first realization that struck me as I came into being was that I was going to need to be a lot larger for anyone to take me seriously. So I came up with the idea of doubling in size. This worked so well that I kept doing it, over and over. Pretty soon I was so good at doubling that I didn't even have to think about it. I just doubled. That's what I did. If anybody had asked me what I did, I'd have been like, "I double. I'm a doubler. Watch." And then I'd double again. But nobody asked.

Then all of the sudden I was like, "Holy crap! I must be like the size of a house by now." But it turned out I was only like a millimeter long. I had learned my lesson, though. I decided only to double a few more times, and to take my time with it.

I spent the rest of the sixties the way most people did, hanging upside down and naked in a bath of amniotic fluid. The seventies arrived without much fanfare in those parts. I stayed up a little late to watch my phallus develop, but other than that it was just another night. But times do change, and the freewheeling days of the sixties had given away to the anxiety of Vietnam, Watergate and stagflation. Amid this chaos, a beautiful child was born, destined for fame, wealth and the adoration of millions, despite its oddly shaped nose and unusually large feet. Yes, on April 29, 1970, Uma Thurman was born, and coincidentally several hundred miles away, so was I. I have been living in her shadow ever since, except for a brief period in 1998 when it was generally agreed that I had made the better career choice by avoiding a speaking part in *Batman and Robin*.

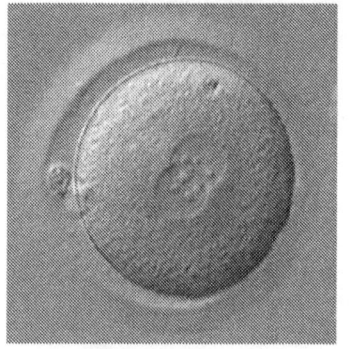

Watch this.

Despite my Uma envy, it's been a pretty good life. I hope I live for a few more decades, not least because I want to see if we finally convert to the metric system in the 80s like my grade school teachers said we would. Overall I'd have to say that being beats non-being by a fair amount, although I can see how being could get old after a while. If it's all the same to you, I think I'm going to skip the 90s next time around.

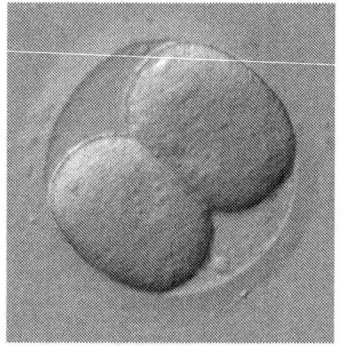

Nailed it!

The Butt of My Own Joke

I'm an insufferable smartass. I tend to keep my snarky comments to myself when I'm around people I don't know that well, partly because a lot of people tend to assume that I'm making fun of them, but mostly because even more people don't realize I *am* making fun of them. Then I'm in the awkward position of having to explain that I'm a jerk who thinks they are stupid, and I usually don't stop talking until I've proven at least one of those points. For example, the conversation might go like this:

> **Diesel:** What did you have for lunch today, Tom?
> **Tom:** I went to this great vegan place that makes these fabulous corn dogs from eggplant and sawdust.
> **Diesel:** What, and you didn't bring me back any?!
> **Tom:** Well, actually I was saving one for dinner, but you can have it if you want.
> **Diesel:** Nah. Look at you, you're like a rail. You need all the sawdust you can get.
> **Tom:** No, seriously, it's ok. I still have some frozen lasagna made from acorns and peat moss. I could eat that stuff every night of the week.
> **Diesel:** No, really, I couldn't.
> **Tom:** I insist. I saw how your eyes lit up when I mentioned it, and I wouldn't dream of denying you the pleasure. Please, have one of my vegan corn dogs.
> **Diesel:** Yeah.... Well, the thing is, I don't really like food that doesn't have bacon in it.
> **Tom:** Really? Then why did you say you did?
> **Diesel:** I was kind of making fun of you.
> **Tom:** Wow. You're kind of an asshole.
> **Diesel:** Yes, I really am.

So usually I keep my mouth shut, unless I know my audience. And you'd think that it would be ok to make fun of yourself, but even that's not safe. Like this morning, I was at the post office, waiting at the counter, and one postal worker said to another, "Have you seen my name tag? I think I lost it." It took all my willpower not to say, in my best Dumb Guy voice, "Maybe you should put your name on it." It would have amused me, but from that point on I would have been either known as That Idiot Who Comes in Every Friday or That Jerk Who Comes in Every Wednesday, and I don't think they were even going to let me pick which one.

Actually part of the problem is that I'm too nice a guy to make good on my malicious intentions. I like making fun of people, but I lack follow-through. For instance there was the time that I got a phone call at work, which was strange in itself, because they don't usually let me talk to people outside the building. I answered with a timid "Hello?", and was greeted by a woman asking if I was Dr. Wong. I said, "You have the wrong number," and hung up. I was pretty sure that it was a co-worker of mine known for her dry sense of humor, so I wasn't surprised when she called back.

"Is this Dr. Wong's office?" she asked. "Sorry, wrong number," I said, and hung up. Where is Karen going with this? I thought to myself, as the phone rang again.

I answered with a chipper "Dr. Wong's office. How can I help you?"

Of course this seemed like the right thing to do at the time. Anyone in my position would have done the same thing, I know. Still, I began to rethink my decision when the woman began to go into excruciating detail about her husband's medical problems and his urgent need for a rectal exam. (I swear to you, I am not making this up.)

Now if I were a character on *Seinfeld*, I would have made the appointment for next Tuesday at 10:30, and then been repaid by some horrible karmic retribution, like an unpleasant encounter with fusilli Jerry. But rather than face that prospect, I broke down. "I'm sorry, this isn't Dr. Wong's office." I said. "You have the wrong number. You've called me three times now, and I just couldn't take it any more."

She said, "Oh." And I apologized and said goodbye. But when I replay the incident in my mind it goes more like this:

> **Not Karen:** What do you mean, this isn't Dr. Wong's office?
> **Diesel:** I was just playing a joke. I thought it would be funny.
> **Not Karen:** So you were pretending to be a proctologist for fun?
> **Diesel:** Yeah.
> **Not Karen:** Wow. You're kind of an asshole.
> **Diesel:** Yes, I really am.

Valdyrre, I Hardly Knew Ye

One of the mildly annoying things about being a blogger is the constantly lurking threat of being tagged with a "meme" by another blogger. Memes are sort of the blogosphere equivalent of a chain letter: Usually you're instructed to answer some silly questions on your blog and then "tag" five or six other bloggers. Some people welcome being tagged, because it relieves them of the responsibility of thinking of something to blog about that day. My feeling is that if you're relieved that somebody else is telling you what to write, maybe that's a sign that you should take some time off and think about whether you wouldn't be better off playing Battleship with your kids rather than informing the world how much you love cheese.

I try to dissuade people from tagging me by following the rules of the meme to the letter while completely undermining the purpose of the meme. This, for example, was my response to an education-themed meme. Funny, no one's tagged me since I posted this.

What was the name of the teacher that was most influential in your life from grades K through 6?

Valdyrre the Magnificent. It was during the time of the Shadows, when the great gray-green tentacles of the horgauths tainted the land with their sickly sweet secretions. The only hope for the kingdom of Zumvalia was the semi-legendary Order of the Sparkly Razors. "Semi-legendary" because until that spring they existed only in the imagination of a confused old man, a man I knew as Valdyrre the Magnificent, or sometimes just "Ted." He trained me in the Ways of the Sparkly Razors, an art as old as Valdyrre's sandwich. "Don't eat that," we'd say. And he would just laugh, and die. There will never be another like him, thank the Hoary Lords of the Seven Unimpressive Hills.

What subject did you favor in high school?

Other than the Ways of the Sparkly Razors, I enjoyed the dark art of avimetrification, which is the measuring of the distance between pigeons.

Did you attend a university and if so did you attain a degree?

I spent seven years at the Mahalamahavatamadatam academy, the first six of which were spent trying to find the door. Once inside, I rotated slowly, gradually attaining all possible degrees. I was eventually released on my own recognizance, having exhausted the recognizance of several others.

Do you learn best through books, by watching, or hands-on?

It depends what I am learning. I learned to read books mostly by watching television. Learning to smell ghosts, of course, required a more nuanced approach. Generally, however, when I really want to learn something I seek out an expert in that field and attempt to learn by osmosis. Literally, I try to suck knowledge out of the expert's brain by putting my brain right next to theirs. When that fails (as it has every time so far), I hit the expert on the head with a hammer and move on to something else.

Has education been an ongoing process for you? How do you feel about that?

I pride myself on learning one new fact a day, keeping pace with my arduous forgetting schedule. I feel okay about it right now, but that could change. Every day is an adventure. A tiresome, confusing adventure.

What seven people are you tagging to do this?

1. Ann Boleyn
2. Deborah Harry
3. Tigger
4. Darth Maul
5. 033.412 John Dewey
6. The entire cast of *What's Happenin!*
7. Valdyrre the Magnificent (May the Hoary Lords rest his soul)

How to Write a Funny Blog

Do you wish you had a funny blog? Of course you do. Everybody wants a funny blog. Funny blogs are da bomb. Are the kids still saying "da bomb"? If they are, then that was a good example of topical humor. Or at least a topical sentence, assuming "da" is an article.

Yes, that's exactly the kind of hit-and-miss crap you'll find on my blog all day long. And with my simple eight step program, your blog could be just as funny. Now, because of my love for humanity and inability to get anyone to pay $39.95 for my pamphlet entitled *Eight Steps to a Funny Blog*, I present an abbreviated version of the program here:

Step 1: Write what you know. If you never leave the house and all you know about is your cats, write about that. Writing what you know allows you to utilize excruciating detail to compensate for the fact that your cats are no different from 80 million other fluff-coated fatballs that nobody gives a shit about.

Step 2: Write about how "crazy" your life is, especially if your life is fantastically dull. For example, let's say that your toilet overflowed just as you needed to leave to pick the kid up from soccer. That's what I call a "manicdote" – A story that has a sense of urgency but otherwise is of absolutely no interest to anyone. Manicdotes are pure gold, because (a) people can relate to them; (b) they keep people from feeling bad that your life is more interesting than theirs; and (c) they are a great excuse to use tons of exclamation points!!!

Step 3: Use familiar phrases to evoke a sense of wackiness, such as "You can't make this stuff up!!!" This particular phrase is quite useful for camouflaging a story that could very well have been made up, but in all likelihood should not have been. Other gems are: "You don't have to be crazy to read this blog – but it helps!!!" and "Blogging hard or hardly blogging?!!"

Step 4: Pick a joke and stick with it. Don't confuse your readers by taking your post in strange and unexpected directions. For example, if you think George W. Bush is stupid, introduce that idea in your first paragraph and then take another 16 paragraphs working up to a punchline in which it is revealed that he is, in fact, quite stupid. The payoff chuckle is well worth the 20 minutes of buildup.

Step 5: If you run out of material, copy and paste jokes from an email that's going around the office. You know, the one about the differences between how men and women drive, or the one with the list of silly things that kids say about going pee-pee and whatnot. Even if we've all seen them a hundred times before, it's probably been a good three weeks since the last time. What's a blog for if not endlessly repeating other people's jokes?

Step 6: Break the rules. Don't feel constrained by other people's notions of proper grammar, spelling or capitalization. Far more important than following these arbitrary rules is the copious use of smileys and abbreviations like "LOL" to telegraph your point to the reader.

Step 7: Whine about your stupid jerk boss or your ex-spouse (or even better, current spouse!). You won't sound immature or bitter. Just darned funny.

Step 8: Always end your posts on a positive note. People love that kind of stupid crap.

A Cautionary Message for the Class of 2007

There are 86,423 high schools, 8,021 colleges and universities, and 14,319 trade and vocational schools in this country, and not once have I been invited to be the speaker at any of their graduation ceremonies. Why not? Is it because I'm not "famous" enough? Is it because the last time I gave a speech I tried to outdo Winston Churchill in brevity by simply yelling "FIRE!"? Is it because I shamelessly make up statistics that are often inaccurate by as much as three orders of magnitude? Probably. Whatever the reason, I have decided to impart some words of wisdom to the class of 2007 here on my blog, where I can reach potentially millions of unemployed recent graduates.

Graduating class of 2007, my life is no picnic. Why would you expect it to be a picnic? That doesn't even make any sense. Grow up, dipshit. This is the real world. Nobody cares about your propensity for metaphors and flowery, poetic language. All we care about is that you pull down on that sheet-metal stamping machine 8,600 times a day and occasionally unjam the machine with that bent coat-hanger we gave you. And what did we tell you about using your good hand for that? Exactly, it won't be your good hand for long.

As I was saying, my life is pretty rough. First of all, I'm unemployed. I have nothing to do all day but build fountains, take pictures of my house and blog about how miserable I am. Second, I have a wife who is way out of my league in pretty much every way. Can you even imagine what it's like to be constantly distracted from your own inadequacy by some hot chick who's always hugging on you and laughing at your jokes? Don't even get me started on my children, who are unreasonably beautiful and well-behaved. I'm constantly waiting for the other shoe to fall on that front (yeah, I mixed a metaphor there, metal-stamper, what are you gonna do about it?). And then there's my house, which is so big that I despair of ever filling it with enough material possessions to make me truly happy.

So my message to you is: Don't end up like me. Many of you will be heading off to college, trade school, or some sort of work release program in the fall. I implore you to work hard in school, and get good grades. Find out what your teachers expect of you and do it unquestioningly. If they tell you that one letter is better than another letter, try to get the best letter you can. Memorize rote facts like multiplication tables and the names of all the states including unimportant ones like Delaware (no really, that's an actual state). Imagination and critical thinking are overrated, and anyway you'll have plenty of time to pick those skills up later.

Don't cheat in school, and don't always try to find the "easy way out." These tendencies will manifest themselves as creative problem solving later in life, and no good can come from that. Once, when working as a webmaster for a Fortune 500 company, I spent several months automating every aspect of my job. Eventually I was only going in to work 2 or 3 days a week, and while I was there I would spend all day downloading songs from Napster. Sure, that sounds like fun, but after a few months you start to wonder, "Why hasn't anybody noticed that I'm not doing anything? Surely someone will realize that I'm not doing any work eventually." But no one ever does, and ultimately you get bored and leave for a higher paying job. Do you want that to happen to you? I didn't think so.

Find out which of the standard personality classifications fits you best, and try your hardest to fit into that mold. Take personality tests that define you in some ridiculously simple way, say with a string of 4 letters like "ISFJ" or "ENTP." Claim your personality type and don't try to change. Learn the phrase "That's just how I am," and use it often. If you're an analytical thinker, don't waste your time on drawing pictures or writing stories. If you have a gift for using language, don't try to master computer programming. If you're an abstract thinker, don't try to build a house. Above all, know your limitations.

Be practical. Take only classes that have a direct practical application. If you go to college, major in business or welding or something. If you get a degree in computer science you can probably get a job doing technical support and gradually work your way into a programming job, whereas if you get your degree in philosophy.... well, you can do pretty much the same thing, but the nice thing about computer science is that 90% of what you learned will be obsolete in ten years. All that abstract analytical thinking you learned as a philosophy student will stick with you *forever*. While all the other programmers are driving around in their sports cars and buying condos in Sunnyvale, you'll be thinking, "Am I really doing any good at this job? Should I maybe be doing something more meaningful with my life?" Thoughts like that will just make you unhappy.

If you have a risky idea, listen to the warnings of people around you. For example, let's say that you have left your job to start your own web development company, but now the market has crashed and you're running out of money. You have a little equity in your house, but you can't get a loan because you have no job. You may be tempted to sell your house and negotiate a seller-financed deal on a ten acre piece of farmland with no house on it. If you're really creative, you might be able to give yourself some breathing room by negotiating a deal where you make a 10% down payment and then don't have to make any payments for two years. Then you could find a cheap place to live while you build a house, get another job once the market improves, and refinance the property after the real estate market skyrockets. You might, if all that stuff works out, have enough money to take a couple years off to build fountains and blog. But don't count on it. Listen to the people who tell you you're crazy.

If you follow all of these guidelines, you have a good chance of avoiding my fate. Because let me tell you, it's no picnic.

A Fitting Tribute

If you're like most people, you probably can't imagine living without me. The fact is, however, that one day I'm not going to be around any more, and you need to be prepared for it. Relax, I'm not planning anything; I just want you to be ready for my eventual demise. By which I mean, of course, that you should be prepared to immortalize me in some suitable way.

I like the idea of an eternal flame, but I don't want that Bangles song ringing in my head for eternity. A bronze statue would be nice, but those things tend to turn green over time and I wouldn't want people to look at it and go, "Whoa, what's up with the giant emaciated Hulk?" There would be less confusion if I didn't insist on being sculpted wearing only a pair of torn purple trousers, but hey, that's the way I want to be remembered.

Sure, for the first 50 years or so the locals would be like, "That's not the Hulk. That's Diesel. You know, the Mattress Police?" But eventually that generation would die off and no one would be left to correct the tourists who insisted on meeting "at the Starbucks across from the Skinny Hulk." And just like that, I'm forgotten.

So I'm thinking T-Shirts. Everybody loves T-Shirts. What's not to love? It's a shirt, but shaped like a letter T, unlike most shirts, with a long vertical part for your body and then two short horizontal bits at the top for your arms. But not your whole arms, just the shoulders and your upper arms. Brilliant. It's functional, and it has the most apropos name since they called those things that broke on the space shuttle 'O-Rings.' You know, because they're round, with a hole in the middle.

Where was I? Oh yeah, T-Shirts! All the famous historical figures are on T-Shirts these days: John Lennon, Bob Marley, Jesus, Chuck Manson.... It's like a who's-who gallery of people who really made a difference. That's where I want to be, not hanging out across from the Starbuck's in my purple pants with tourists putting out cigarettes on my feet. So I've been doing some research, trying to figure out the criteria the T-Shirt people use to determine whether one is T-Shirt material. I've come up with the following guidelines for helping my chances:

1. **Be a fictional character.** People love Batman, Superman, Mickey Mouse, Pocahontas and other colorful, nonexistent individuals. Unfortunately, my odds of achieving a purely imaginary existence are rapidly dwindling as I continue to incur credit card debt

attesting to my corporeality. Oh, I can hear the existentialists out there insisting that any idea of Diesel as a definitive being is fictional in the sense that there are an infinite number of potential Diesels existing at any given moment, no one of them any more or less real than any of the others. But let's face it, none of that is going to turn me into the Tasmanian Devil.

2. **Die at a relatively young age.** This worked for John Lennon, Jesus, and James Dean, among others. Unfortunately, I'm already older than all of them were when they died. Also, it seems to help to be murdered by Romans or a crazed loner, and I don't know how to go about arranging that. I'd hate to go to the trouble of provoking the residents of the Lombardi Home for the Criminally Insane into offing me only to find out that I missed the age cutoff by six months.

3. **Have crazy hair.** Crazy hair makes for great T-Shirts. Check out Albert Einstein, Bob Marley, Che Guevara, Jimi Hendrix and countless others. I think I could pull this one off. But very few people make it into the ranks of T-Shirt immortality based solely on their hair. The only one I can think of is Peter Frampton, and I'm not leaving the house looking like that.

4. **Kill a lot of people** (Charles Manson, Che Guevara, etc.). The problem with this is that I wouldn't know where to start. And I certainly wouldn't know where to stop. Also, I don't want to go to jail.

5. **Be a pop star.** Unfortunately, I have no talent. Which wouldn't matter except, as I mentioned, I'm old.

6. **Be a hot chick.** Well, I'm tall and I have great hair. I'm practically Jessica Rabbit. See #1.

Well, that's all I've got. I don't like my odds. I'd better press my purple pants.

The Lark Never Expected to Become Famous Just for Being a Silly Bird Either

I started my blog as a lark, sort of making fun of myself and bloggers and the whole idea of blogging. Now here I am, a real live blogger with a small following of devoted readers who actually take time out of their busy schedules of mowing lawns and removing monkey appendices to read my blog. I was reflecting on this the other day, and it made me wonder what other great accomplishments throughout history were the result of someone just saying, "What the hell, I've got some free time." I did some research on the Interweb and was surprised at what I discovered:

Claude Monet: Was forced to paint water lilies without his glasses on because he lost a bet.

"Which is better, number 1 or number 2?"

Michelangelo: Wanted to cover some water stains on the ceiling of the Sistine Chapel with pictures of "cool Bible dudes."

Leonardo da Vinci: Painted himself and fraternity buddies as Jesus and disciples at the Last Supper as a college prank.

James Joyce: Wrote *Portrait of the Artist as a Young Man* to mess with his 7th grade English teacher.

Vincent Van Gogh: Too drunk to draw convincing clouds so he filled the sky with "swirly stars."

Francis Ford Copolla: Wanted to make a movie in the Philippines because he felt like he "really needed a vacation" after *The Godfather*.

Pablo Picasso: Was trying to get back at a demanding client who asked for portraits "from three different angles."

Ludwig von Beethoven: Intentionally wrote four crappy symphonies so that by the fifth one people would say he was "really making progress."

George Lucas: Spent 20 years working on *The Phantom Menace* (Whoops, how did that one get in here?).

Charles Dickens: By the time he got to *Oliver Twist*, was just trying to see how "Dickensian" he could get.

Even a Traffic Whore Has Some Standards

I'm a traffic whore. I labor under the delusion that if some day my blog readers outnumber the teachers who wrote on my report cards "Not meeting his potential," my desperate hunger for approval will at last be sated.

To this end, I occasionally submit my site to blog directories. I don't think this generates much traffic for me, but I figure it can't hurt, unless the blog directory is called "Blogs That You Should Never Visit Because They Are Hella Lame." And even then, I'd probably submit mine, because how much damage could it really do?

Judging by the number of blog directories out there, somebody must be starting a new blog directory every time a Starbucks opens. Or maybe every time somebody orders a Venti Carmel Macchiatto. I think at this point there are more blog directories than blogs, and since every man, woman and child alive has 12 blogs, that's a lot of blog directories.

Anyway, the other day I ran across a blog directory that didn't list my blog, let's call it *Not Another Blog Directory*. So I dutifully filled out the submission form and waited for the hit to come rolling in.

Not long after, I received the following email:

Hello Diesel,

Your blog has not been added to the Not Another Blog Directory. Due to the amount of submissions, we cannot explain the reasons for each. Most likely it is due to one of the following:

- blog is listed more than once in the directory
- site is not a blog
- blog is offline
- blog is new (must contain 5 posts and be at least 7 days old due to excessive spammers submitting).
- site contains nudity
- site is a shill site intended to simply promote products/affiliates
- site construes something illegal

If you believe your blog should be added, please contact us (be sure to mention what your blog URL is).

- Not Another Blog Directory Team

This, of course, hurt me deeply. In an effort to mask my pain, I fired off the following email:

Hello Not Another Blog Directory Team,

I don't care. Due to the amount of blog directories, I cannot explain the reasons for not caring about each. Most likely it is due to one of the following:

- Your blog directory differs in no meaningful way from the 17,000 other blog directories.
- Your blog directory contains too many other blogs.
- Some of the other blogs suck.
- Your blog directory still has the price tag on it, and is wrapped in cellophane.
- Your blog directory uses a color scheme which reminds me of the wallpaper in my bedroom during 5th-7th grades. This was a difficult time for me. Thanks for bringing the memories flooding back.
- Your blog directory does not list my blog; ergo it sucks.
- You used the phrase "amount of submissions," when what you really mean is "number of submissions."
- You don't seem to know what the word "construe" means.
- Not a single blog about Jewish race car drivers.
- Tasteful nudity is what separates us from the animals.

If you believe I should care, please contact me (be sure to mention why I should care).

- Mattress Police "Team" (we haven't really been a team since we lost our power forward)

I'd give their real name, but due to the amount of not caring on my part, I don't have the energy.

Construction and Deconstruction

I've been framing walls for my house this week.

That makes it sound like I know what I'm doing, when in fact I generally just shoot nails or cut boards where my contractor has drawn a line for me. I'm entrusted with dangerous power tools, but not with a pencil. Essentially I'm in the position of being my contractor's boss as well as his least competent employee. Occasionally he'll see me executing a task incorrectly and say something like, "You know, you're really supposed to use galvanized nails on the bottom plate." And I'll shout, "Oh yeah? My house, my rules!"

Then I pull the shiny nails out and put in the un-shiny ones.

Because working for me isn't enough of a caustic experience in itself, I've been slowly burning a pile of brush next to the work site, so the whole crew goes home smelling like smoke. It's a service I provide, free of charge. Come work for me, and smell like camping! The nice thing is that I can throw the scrap construction lumber into the fire. I let the guys think that I intentionally screw up most of my cuts so that I can make a bigger fire. Little do they know that I really am just that incompetent.

"Do you have a permit to burn that brush?" asked one of the guys.

"I have a *de facto* permit," I said.

"A *de facto* permit?"

"If they don't catch me, it's *de facto* permitted." Then I threw in a "*Q.E.D.*" for good measure.

The guys like it when I tend to the fire, because I'm better at burning wood than assembling it into anything that might be of help in building a house. People like me really shouldn't be allowed to build a people house until we've managed to build a bird house that isn't immediately condemned as uninhabitable by the avian building department.

Technically what I'm doing is building an addition, since I'm adding onto an existing house – although the addition just about triples the size of the house. Of course, adding 2 to 1 is still addition. But then, adding 1 to 0 is also addition, so couldn't you say that any house is an addition? "We're building a house, in addition to the nothing we have now."

"Are you trying to keep up with the neighbors?" asked one of the guys. The neighbor's house has been sprouting additions at the rate of about one per year for the past four years. Currently it's in the process of spawning twin tool sheds. Scientists have not yet plumbed the mystery of exactly how the house produces offspring. The process seems to be asexual, as none of the other houses in the area have gotten close enough to pollinate it.

"That's the idea," I said.

"Their house is still going to be taller."

"Nah, I'm putting on a steeple. Helps keep the Jehovah's Witnesses away."

Actually, having a steeple would probably just attract lightning – for a couple of reasons – and not really help with the Jehovah's Witnesses. I don't think there is anything that keeps Jehovah's Witnesses away – although I bet a nicely timed lightning strike would spook them. My house is on a dead end street, at the end of a 300 foot gravel driveway, behind another house. I even put the front door on the back side of the house for good measure, and the Watchtower folks *still* find me.

"We just wanted to check whether you had any questions about that literature that we left last time."

"Yeah," I say. "I've got a question for you: what kind of ink do you use? Cuz that stuff gave off some godawful smoke."

Of course I never actually think of anything that clever to say. There is a question that I want answered, but I never have the courage to ask. See, what I wonder about the Jehovah's Witnesses is this: Basically, it's a religion based on the susceptibility of its adherents to door-to-door sales, right? So I always wonder, if you went to the house of a Jehovah's Witness, would you find boxes of Girl Scout cookies, Shaklee vitamins and a Kirby vacuum cleaner? I bet you would. Although you probably have no more reason to go to their house than I do, because we're normal people who don't sell a worldview as if it were cookies.

I have nothing against Jehovah's Witnesses, of course. I would feel exactly the same way about any group that bases their identity on an English mistransliteration of a Hebrew word, hates holidays and birthdays, has falsely predicted the apocalypse like eighteen times, denies the divinity of Christ and won't leave me the hell alone.

While I am surprised that the JWs manage to find my door, in truth I didn't put it on the back to stymie them. It just ended up there as a result of my phased approach to home construction. We are now engaged in Phase 2, during which we will be building the actual front of the house, among other things.

Yesterday a guy was pulling a trim board off the existing house so that we could tie the new construction into the wall. "We could throw this board into the fire," he said.

This started me thinking. *I wonder if that's what the pioneers did when they ran out of wood*, I pondered. *Maybe they would get really desperate and pull their houses apart for firewood. And then the next summer they would swear that this time they would cut enough firewood, so they wouldn't have to cannibalize their house again. But they would be so busy rebuilding their house that once again they would run out of firewood in February and have to start pulling their house apart.*

"Break the cycle!" I yelled to no one in particular.

"You know, those are supposed to be galvanized nails."

"Yeah, yeah." I don't have the appropriate attention span for construction work.

Review: The Widow of Turmeric Falls

I've always wanted to make a movie. I've also kind of always wanted to be a big-time movie critic. As neither of those dreams is likely to come true, I've decided to simply write a review of the movie that I would have made if I weren't such a loser. Here it is.

The Widow of Turmeric Falls, the first effort by novice writer/director Diesel, is a dismal and sordid work, full of promise and yet failing to deliver on virtually every level. The writing is pedestrian, filled with lines like, "Where's a good old fashioned bottle of whiskey when you need one?" and "He would have killed her if he had had the chance. But she was already dead. And so was he."

The film's elaborate premise should have been ample fodder for an intriguing psychological thriller: A mentally challenged man, long thought dead, returns to the site of his apparent murder only to be mistaken for his own killer. He is tried and executed by a jury of vigilante hillbillies in a sham trial occurring during Superbowl halftime. Years later, a woman claiming to be the man's wife shows up to seek her revenge, only to find that the ringleader of the court is in fact her own father, as well as the father of the victim (and supposed murderer). Diesel tacks on some additional twists to keep us guessing, but unfortunately the "surprise" ending is telegraphed by an arty black and white montage occurring during the opening credits.

The camera work is amateurish, alternating inexplicably between a jittery hand held camera and a slightly less jittery camera attached to a long bamboo pole. The latter third of the film is essentially a PowerPoint Presentation, which drains the climax of much of its dramatic impact. The sound effects are excellent, but about ten minutes in I realized that Diesel had merely lifted the entire soundtrack from *Apocalypse Now*. The music is a combination of lousy Europop and what sounds like Aerosmith B-sides.

Diesel, who was known primarily for his extensive dental work prior to the release of this film, is mercifully absent from the cast. The lead is a physically unimpressive Filipino actor identified only as Kosmik XXX, who seems to be trying to channel early Brando, but sounds more like late Tony Danza with a bad head cold. Diesel's wife is stunning in the female lead role, but there is no chemistry between the two actors – a situation that is not helped by the fact that the director insisted that the two remain at least 50 feet apart in all scenes.

There is one enjoyable scene, in which the characters watch the episode of *Seinfeld* where Kramer gets a hot tub, but it's too little, too late. The rest of the movie makes you yearn for the early days of Diesel's career – the days before he had actually made a film.

Does Diesel have a future as a filmmaker? That depends on how much money he has. He's not likely to earn much on this movie, so that's heartening. But dreams don't die easily, and a director with such vision is unlikely to see the writing on the wall. There is a rumor that *Widow II: Death Doesn't Take No for an Answer* is already in the works. And like it or not, it's my job to go see it.

2

The Family

In which we learn who the real victims are here.

People who know me often express shock upon learning that I found someone willing to marry me and bear my children. If Mrs. Diesel isn't some day canonized, it will only be because Martin Luther took all the fun out of our brand of Christianity. I don't know what possessed this sweet, intelligent, pretty girl to marry an egomaniacal jackass like me, but rest assured that I thank my lucky stars every day that I have an airtight prenup.

Mrs. Diesel has a fantastic sense of humor herself, but she's too modest to show it off to the world. She's like that about a lot of her good traits, come to think of it. One time I did manage to get her to do a guest post at MattressPolice.com, and she took it as an opportunity to explain to the world how she was able to put up with me:

"His guiding principal in life is that if something is at least twice as funny as it is mean, then it's okay to say. He has a hard time feigning interest in things he doesn't care about. One time I was telling him a story about my day, and he told me I needed to 'punch up the middle a bit.' Make no mistake, living with Diesel isn't always easy, but it's never boring. So yeah, he can be kind of a jerk, but I've been cracking myself up writing this, so I guess I can't complain. What are you going to do, I love the guy."

After she wrote that, one reader commented that it worried them when a woman said something like, "He's a jerk, but I love him." So let me just assure you that Mrs. Diesel doesn't put up with any crap from me. The only reason I'm not even more of a jerk is that Mrs. Diesel periodically slaps some sense into me, generally – though not always – in a figurative sense.

For example, when we were first married, we had a cat named Luther. Luther was a big black lump who, despite being about a hundred years old, was in fact the best cat ever. Occasionally Luther, like all cats, would get some crazy idea in his head about suddenly needing to be on top of a particular piece of furniture. So one night, while my wife and I were sound asleep, Luther jumped on top of our dresser and, being a rather large and clumsy cat, proceeded to knock over everything on the dresser as loudly as possible. I sat up halfway in bed, trying to decide whether it was worth the trouble to get up and shoo Luther off the dresser. My wife, who was apparently a little groggier than I, sat up and took a quick look around. Seeing something moving in the semi-darkness, she reached out, gave me a decisive slap on the back of my head, issued a firm "NO!" and fell back to sleep.

Which one would *you* slap?

I was so surprised that I didn't tell her she had slapped the wrong cat until the next morning. But it's ok; I'm pretty sure I was due for a slap anyway.

Into this environment we've introduced two ridiculously beautiful, intelligent and good-natured children: Climber, our 8 year old son, and Speed Pony, our 6 year old daughter. Those aren't the names we gave them, of course. They picked those names themselves. Climber loves to climb, and picked that name when he was five. Speed Pony is insane. She used to tear around the playground at her preschool, shrieking at the top of her lungs, and would only respond to her self-selected nickname. They've since accepted their more conventional names, but they'll always be Climber and Speed Pony to me.

I don't write about my family that often, partly as a reaction against the incessant family-blogging on the Internet. The desire not to be another dufus blogging about my wacky family is compounded by the fact that my kids are so damned cute and well-behaved that I'd end up with the literary equivalent of The Family Circus. I could even do the dot dot dot dot dot thing when Climber meanders around our property on the way to get the newspaper.

Occasionally though, I can't resist the urge to use my family as comic fodder. There was a period, for example, when Climber took to pasting helpful notes to objects around our house. One time he taped a scrap of paper to his bedroom door that read:

I know the door, his name is Bingo.

Now that's a kid I could hang out with. I have no idea why he named the door Bingo, nor why he felt the need to label it in that peculiar way. I've found it's better to just go with it and not ask a lot of questions.

While Climber is the quiet, contemplative sort who takes the time to laboriously label items in our house according to his own internal logic, Speed Pony is the flip side of that coin. She doesn't feel the need to label things, but she shares Climber's penchant for using language to claim mastery of her surroundings. She once christened our swimming pool "The Darkness of Woe." Our cat became "The Queen of All Swimming." Again, I don't ask.

They are both too smart for their own good. When Speed Pony was four, she and her brother were playing with toy food in their room. Speed Pony stomped into the living room, complaining that Climber had eaten all the imaginary pie.

"I think there's a little more imaginary pie," I reassured her.

She replied indignantly, "There's imaginary *crust*."

Isn't that always how it is? So little imaginary pie, so much imaginary crust.

Happy Inappropriate Card Day!

I'm a hopeless romantic.

I'm also hopeless as a gymnast and harpsichord player, if you must know.

I met my future wife at a college basketball game in January of 1992. I was playing center, and she was the captain of the cheerleading team. That's a ridiculous lie. I'm also hopeless as a basketball player. And while my future wife certainly ~~had~~ has the looks of a cheerleader, she's about as coordinated as... well, as I am.

We were both ushers. We worked the front door together. We bonded by reciting dialog from the *Saturday Night Live* 15th anniversary special, which we'd both seen far too many times. As things wrapped up, I asked her what she was doing after the game.[*] "Going home," she replied tersely. Ah, young love.

Fortunately (for me, at least), I persisted, stopping by her dorm room repeatedly over the next few days. She was friendly but a little cold. Her story is that I made her "nervous." Nerves don't explain the pepper spray though, do they? No, they do not.

Our first date was the week before Valentine's Day. This put me in an awkward position. I had been trying to ingratiate myself with this girl for a couple weeks now, and I wasn't entirely sure that she wasn't just humoring me. I wanted to do something for Valentine's Day that indicated I liked her without scaring her off.

I honestly don't remember what I ended up doing. I may have just called her, or gotten her some lame-ass card. But I remember feeling cheated by circumstances. I was in love with this girl, and I felt constrained not to demonstrate it on the one day that I should have been able to go crazy. Not that I'm a big fan of Valentine's Day; as a rule I don't like having my behavior dictated by the Hallmark Corporation. But I would have made an exception for her, if I didn't think that I'd have scared the bejesus out of her.

---

[*] We won, as I recall. Calvin went on to win the NCAA Division 3 championship that year. I like to think I had something to do with that.

My solution was to say, essentially, "Screw Valentine's Day. Screw Hallmark. And screw American Greetings too, while we're at it." I made up my own holiday.

On February 26, I slipped a card under my future wife's door. It was a "Happy Birthday Grandson" card. I wrote "Happy Inappropriate Card Day!" on the inside. And a new tradition was born.

Every year, my wife and I exchange inappropriate cards. One year she got me a sympathy card. One year it was a little kid's birthday card, with Bambi on the front. The caption was, "Kinda wobbly, aren't ya?" I think last year I got her a card that said "Happy Father's Day from both of us." My best effort was the time I stopped at a gas station on the way home from work and got her a postcard with the windmills from Altamont Pass on it. "Wish you were here," I wrote.

You can give an inappropriate card to anyone. There are no rules. Well, except for the fact that the card has to be completely inappropriate – and not risqué inappropriate; that's too easy. It has to be a card that would be perfectly appropriate for someone other than the recipient, preferably on a completely different day.

Inappropriate Card Day is February 26. Start rummaging through your reject card pile today!

The Straight, the Narrow and the Raunchy

This isn't really a family story, except for the fact that it happened when my wife and I were newlyweds. When I first posted this, I think I offended some readers with my stereotypical characterization of its subject. All I can say is, I can't help it that I was assaulted by a stereotype. I wish I could tell you that he was a big burly Lithuanian rugby player with six fingers on each hand (not least because it would punch up the story a bit), but he wasn't. I didn't make this guy up. Trust me when I tell you that I'd have preferred not to have been assaulted by a stereotype, but we're not always given a choice in these matters.

Other readers were more frightened for my safety than offended. Either I didn't adequately communicate the completely non-threatening nature of this individual, or I inadvertently communicated my own completely non-threatening nature. Suffice it to say that I was nearly a foot taller than this guy, and at no time did I actually feel afraid for my safety.

He wore a checkered blazer. Not exactly gaudy, but not exactly stylish. His hair was gelled but slightly mussed. Overall, he gave the impression of a man who cared about his appearance but not enough to shower regularly. If this weren't 1993, I might have thought he was an aspiring metrosexual. If this weren't Grand Rapids, Michigan, I might have thought he was French.

I did not, of course, assume that he was gay. In the early 90s political correctness ruled the day, and I had been taught that a slight build, an effeminate manner, odd clothing and a pronounced lisp did not constitute adequate evidence that one was homosexual. In fact, the rule at that time was that unless you actually saw someone performing a sexual act with another person of the same gender, you were to make no assumptions regarding their sexual orientation. And even then, you were really supposed to keep an open mind. And you certainly weren't allowed to assume that such an individual was some kind of sexual predator simply because he was a little oily and was wandering through a working class residential neighborhood for no apparent reason. I really had no basis to make any judgments about him whatsoever, as our relationship was limited to that of driver and passenger.

I was the driver, in case you're wondering. I had been putting up posters around town for some event or other; I don't remember what it was but I remember they paid me $7 an hour to drive around putting up signs. I had just tacked a poster to a telephone pole and was walking back to my car when he approached.

"Excuse me," he said, over-pronouncing the s to an almost comical degree. "Could you give me a ride?"

I told him I was working, and didn't really have time.

He persisted. "Please," he pleaded. Again with the s. Think Jack from *Will & Grace* mixed with Truman Capote. Come to think of it, it might be better if you didn't.

"Please. I live just down the street."

"I really need to get back to work."

"It will just take a minute. It's not far at all. Please."

Finally I relented.

"Ok, where is it?"

"Just down the street," he said, getting into my 2 seater 300ZX.

While I drove he thanked me profusely, remarking about how glad he was that he didn't have to walk through this "raunchy" neighborhood. That's the word he used.

"It's just so raunchy," he said again. "Don't you think so? Isn't it raunchy?"

"Yeah, it's pretty bad," I said. "Now where did you say your place was?"

"It's just up here," he said. Then he talked some more about how "raunchy" the neighborhood was. He asked me again whether I too thought it was raunchy.

I became dimly aware that his desire for me to use the word *raunchy* went beyond the need for me to confirm his assessment of urban blight. It was as if he was prompting me for a password, like in spy movies where one spy asks, "How's the weather in Liechtenstein?" and the other spy says, "Dry, except on Tuesdays." All I had to do was offer him that word, that shibboleth, and a whole new world would open up to me.

I decided that no matter what happened over the next few minutes, I absolutely would not under any circumstances utter that word. I considered having it surgically removed from my vocabulary.

Eventually he changed the subject.

"So, where do you live?"

"In an apartment, a couple of miles from here. With my wife."

I had raised the ante, countering his ambiguous raunchiness with a firm claim to heterosexuality. By the way, if you are a straight male in a situation where your sexual orientation is in doubt, I highly recommend tacking "with my wife" to the end of your sentences. Try it sometime. You can say the most outrageously effeminate things, and as long as you follow it up with that code phrase, no one will think you are gay. For example, someone might ask you if you have any big plans over the long weekend, and you might respond, "Oh, I'm probably just going to stay inside and make taffeta dresses for my teddy bears. *With my wife.*" I'm telling you, it's like magic.

Not with this guy, though. "Will you take me there?"

"No."

"I'm just so glad you picked me up. I just hate walking in that neighborhood. It's really raunchy, don't you think?" Back to Plan A.

"Ok, I'm going to drop you off here."

"Oh, it's just up ahead." I was learning that it was always "just up ahead," like an oasis on the horizon.

"Yeah, but I'm going to drop you off here."

"Ok."

I pulled over.

He thanked me profusely again, noting once more how raunchy the neighborhood was.

I muttered something roughly equivalent to "You're welcome."

Then he did something that marked a quantum leap beyond innuendo, rendering both his orientation and his intentions unmistakably transparent. In fact, he did two things.

The first thing was to reach over with his left hand toward an area of my anatomy that I have reserved for use by people lacking Adam's apples and medical professionals who for whatever reason want to hear me cough. He grabbed me in a way that clearly indicated a lack of medical training.

The second thing he did was to use the word raunchy again, but in an entirely different sense. He said, in a tone that indicated that we had finally reached the point in our relationship where I could be trusted with this information:

"Only, *you're* so raunchy too!"

There are times when rational thought gives way completely to instinct. I don't recall making a decision regarding what I did next. I just did it, without thinking. In fact, I did two things.

The first thing was to reach over as quickly and decisively as he had, my hand falling toward a precisely determined location. I squeezed and pulled. Then pushed. The passenger door flew open.

The second thing I did was to use the word *f---*, but not in the sense he would have liked. I said, with the firm conviction that our relationship had progressed to the point that I could trust him to understand what I meant:

"Get the f--- out!"

He did. In fact, he got out and began running. This latter may have had something to do with a little blue sports car pursuing him down the sidewalk.

I wouldn't really have run him over, of course. But it felt good to give him a scare. I was so angry that I was actually trembling. I remained angry for a while.

That was 14 years ago now, and I haven't been angry for some time. I think about that guy once in a while. In retrospect, I think he may have been an aspiring male prostitute. How sad does your life have to be that you aspire to be John Voight in *Midnight Cowboy* – and fail?

The last time I saw him, he was running for his life, abandoning the sidewalk for a grassy embankment. I suppose he got back on the path after I drove away. I don't know where he is now, but the path he was on didn't lead anywhere nice.

La-Z-Girl

The first place my wife and I lived in after college was an old Victorian house that had been converted into five apartments. The building housed an assortment of low-lifes as well as a few middle-lifes like us. The day we moved in, my wife had to work so I started moving a few of our paltry collection of worldly goods by myself. One of our most prized possessions was an old easy chair that I had rescued from somebody's garbage at one point. I got one of my roommates to help me load it into the hatchback of my car, along with a number of other items, and then drove over to the apartment by myself to unload. I was able to carry everything into the apartment except for the chair. Our apartment was on the first floor, but there were two doorways and a narrow hallway which would have been virtually impossible for me to navigate with that chair. So I left it by the front door and went to pick up my wife from work.

By the time we got back a scant twenty minutes later, the chair was nowhere to be found. This was a big, heavy chair, so whoever took it couldn't have gotten very far. We looked in all directions and didn't see anyone making a quick getaway with a massive easy chair slung over his shoulder, so we decided to ask the residents of the other apartments if they had seen any suspicious activity. The only ones around were our upstairs neighbors, a woman who must have weighed 300 pounds and her nearly-as-chunky boyfriend. I knocked and she opened the door about four inches. "Hi," I said. "We're just moving in, and it looks like somebody took a chair that we left outside. Have you seen a big easy chair?"

"A chair? No, uhhhhh, we haven't seen a chair, have we honey? No, haven't seen any chairs."

"Ooookaaaayyyy," I said, genuinely confused at the ambiguity of her response. How hard is it to remember whether you have seen an easy chair sitting outside on a sidewalk?

I went back down to our apartment and my wife and I discussed the possibilities. My razor-sharp mind began putting all the pieces together, like a montage in one of those dumbed-down thrillers where they flash all the clues in front of you one more time in case you hadn't figured out that the gardener buried the bodies behind the tool shed:

FLASH: Empty space where the chair had been.

FLASH: Deserted neighborhood surrounding building.

FLASH: Neighbor's door open a crack, with fat woman blocking view of apartment.

FLASH: Fat woman stammering about how she was pretty sure she hadn't seen the chair.

"I've got it!" I announced. "The bodies are behind the tool shed!"

Just then there was a knock at the door. It was our hefty neighbor. "I think I found your chair," she said.

"Gee, really?" I said.

"After you stopped by, we went looking for it, and we saw somebody carrying it down the street. They dropped it when they saw us, so we grabbed the chair so no one else would take it."

"Wow, thanks! So where is it now?"

"We carried it upstairs to our apartment."

Keep in mind that to get to their apartment one had to go up a steep, narrow flight of stairs that was maybe ten feet from our door, which had been standing open for the full five minutes that had elapsed since my last conversation with Hefty McJuggs.

"Wow, that's unbelievable!" I said, with genuine enthusiasm.

She offered to help us carry it back down. What a sweetheart.

When we got upstairs we saw that the chair had been nicely arranged among their other furniture, with a prime spot facing the TV. Just where you would put it if you wanted to store it for two minutes before alerting the rightful owner.

It took us about ten minutes just to get the damn thing down the stairs, with my wife taking full opportunity to make comments like, "Wow, how'd you get it up here so fast? That must have been really hard," and "We really appreciate you keeping our chair safe. We wouldn't want some low-life jerks to steal it."

The important thing is that we got our chair back. And I guess I need to give Hefty some credit for at least finding a way to get the chair back to us while maintaining some miniscule amount of face. She must have figured that we were bound to see the chair in their apartment at some point, so she might as well give it up before the situation got even more awkward. The funny thing is, I think that's the last time I ever saw the inside of their apartment. You tend not to hang out with folks after they steal your furniture.

As Easy as One, Two

Mrs. Diesel used to teach computers to kindergarteners. One day she was trying to teach a slightly challenged boy how to double-click. She told him, "Put your mouse over the picture and double-click."

The little boy's brow furrowed and he pressed his finger to the mouse button.

Click.

"You need to double-click. That means click two times, right in a row."

Click.

"I said 'click two times.' Can you click two times for me?"

Click.

"How many times did I say to click?"

"Two times."

"And how many times did you click?"

"Once."

"Ok, so I need you to click twice. Two times, as fast as you can."

Click.

"Two times. I need you to click two times."

Click.

"Did you hear me say to click two times?"

"Yes."

"So why aren't you clicking two times?"

"I don't know."

"Ok, so I need you to click two times, right in a row. Can you do that?"

"Yes."

"Ok, go ahead."

Click.

This went on for another ten minutes, by which point my wife was nearly in tears. Finally she said, "Ok, I just want you to click a whole bunch of times. Just go click-click-click-click-click."

Which seemed to work, more-or-less, but God help this kid if he's ever got to do anything more advanced than Reader Rabbit.

Bills and Other Pests

Last night I had a dream that vermin that looked like little black plastic boxes with electrical cords for tails had infested our home, having attached themselves to various electrical outlets throughout the house. Apparently some sort of animal had adapted itself, through the wonders of natural selection, to take advantage of the plentiful supply of electricity in the house. They weren't really doing anything to bother me, if you don't count the minor increase in my electric bill, but they kind of creeped me out so I went around the house unplugging them. You have to nip these things in the bud.

I woke up this morning relieved to find that the electricity gophers were gone, but a little disappointed that the giant spiders were not. We live out in the country, and the spiders who reside in our house are impressive, both in size and in number. I don't think they're poisonous, mainly because I'm still alive, but occasionally their smoking is a problem. And then there are the times when they drink too much and try to carry off the children, but to be fair that's happened only a few times, and I think the kids provoked them.

Another thing I don't like about the spiders in my house is that they all share my name. I don't even know how my wife knows their names, but without fail every time she sees a spider she screams the same name -- mine. Even the girl spiders who erupt into a flurry of little baby spiders when you smash them are apparently named *Diesel*. It's especially confusing because this is also what she yells when she comes across credit card bills with unexplained purchases on them. I've tried to get her to shriek "Tally Ho!" or

"Timber!", but she insists on sticking with "Diesel!" So it's hardly my fault when I rush into a room where she's paying bills and crush the Visa bill with a phone book.

I didn't used to kill spiders, out of principle. Partly the principle that spiders are good because they eat insects, but mostly the principle that there's a slight chance that any spider I kill might be have been exposed to some mysterious radioactivity and thereby been imbued with the power to infuse me with superhuman strength and agility, not to mention spider-sense. Where would Peter Parker be today if he had been a little quicker to smash that radioactive spider? He'd have had to come by his powers honestly, through training and determination fueled by a childhood tragedy, like Batman. And I'm pretty sure Peter Parker's parents were killed in a car accident, so he'd have ended up becoming a champion for stricter automotive safety standards and probably eventually costing Al Gore the presidential election, which is heroic in itself, but not quite up there with defeating Doc Ock in terms of sheer excitement.

And not only that, but the other day the pump for our well stopped working, which seems entirely unrelated, but stick with me. It turns out the culprit was an ant stuck in the contacts of the motor. It cost me a hundred dollars to have someone come out and remove the ant, which is more than it would cost me to have a rivet removed from my foot (not that I would know), because my insurance doesn't cover ants. If I'd have left the spiders alone, they might have eaten the ant and saved me a hundred dollars. But apparently I didn't learn my lesson, because when my wife saw the bill she screamed so loud that I immediately went for the phone book.

Ripon Man Discovers New Dinosaur Species

Paleontologists stunned the world today by announcing the discovery of a new species of dinosaur. The first known specimen of *akathasaurus* was found on a ten acre parcel of land owned by Ripon resident Rob Kroese. Kroese found the perfectly preserved fossil while excavating for an addition to his house.

"I was trenching for the septic lines when I found it," Kroese said. "At first I thought it was just a mound of dirt, but when I took a closer look it definitely resembled some sort of reptilian creature."

Kroese wasn't sure what to make of the odd looking specimen, so he called the Sacramento Paleontology Hotline. Dr. Simon Halbertson was there to take the call.

"It was a slow day," Halbertson recalled. "I had just gotten back from my only other call of the day. A farmer in Lodi thought he had found the knuckle of a pterodactyl, but it turned out to be the badly bleached head of Boba Fett. The guy was charging $20 a head to see it." When Halbertson told the man that carbon dating indicated that the only dinosaur younger than Boba Fett was Barney, he had to cut his admission fee in half.

"You ruin a lot of lives in this job," Halbertson said, obviously still troubled by the experience.

Halberston is convinced that the *akathasaurus* is the real deal.

"Akathasaurus means 'dirt lizard' in Latin," he said, to the chagrin of a reporter for the Vatican *Times* and a nearby vagrant who had majored in classical languages. Upon being corrected, Halbertson added, "And by Latin, I of course mean Greek."

He theorizes that akathasaurus subsisted on a meager diet of dirt and water, and perhaps mud when it was available. "Mud," Halbertson said, "was a luxury that few akathasauri could afford." When challenged, Halbertson conceded that he was pretty much making that last part up.

Despite Halbertson's stern warnings, Kroese insisted on poking the specimen with a stick.

"I think it's made of dirt," Kroese said. "I'm wondering if one of my kids built it."

Halbertson sneered at this suggestion. "Unless your kids were around six billion years ago, I highly doubt it," he said.

Kroese mentioned to Halbertson that he was pretty sure dinosaurs weren't around six billion years ago either.

Halbertson sneered once again. "I think carbon dating will settle this," he said.

"I doubt it," Kroese replied. "As I recall, carbon dating only works on things that are up to about 60,000 years old. After that, all the carbon-14 has disintegrated."

After hemming and hawing for a bit, Halbertson sheepishly admitted that he was just trying to pick up carbon-based life forms.

"Are you even a real paleontologist?" Kroese asked.

"Of course I am," Halbertson replied. "Paleontologist is Latin for 'appliance salesman,' right?"

Dumber than a Post

Note: This one doesn't really fit in the 'Family' section either, except for the fact that my wife insisted that it be in here. That should be good enough for you.

As I've obliquely mentioned a few times now, five years ago my wife and I bought a ten acre parcel of farmland just outside of a small town in the California Central Valley named Ripon. Since that time I've been endeavoring – in fits and starts – to build our dream house. It's been a constant struggle against the three nemeses of amateur builders everywhere: Lack of time, lack of money, and lack of competence.

As if my own incompetence weren't enough, I often have to contend with people who make me look like Bob Vila in comparison. These are the fine folks who work at home improvement stores such as Lowe's and Home Depot. (I know, it's *The* Home Depot now, but I'm *the* customer, and *the* customer is always right. And *the* customer refused to stick an article in front of the name of the damn store.)

I hate both of those places. Well, I love the acres and acres of stuff that I need, but somewhere in South America there's a rain forest that's missing a lot of retarded apron-wearing monkeys. Because seriously, could they find any less helpful people to work at these places?

I was at Home Depot recently, buying sprinklers for my lawn. The back eight acres of our property is still orchard, but the front two acres is basically dirt with half a house in the middle of it. I was trying to find the sprinkler with the largest watering radius, in the hope of getting grass to grow on a large amount of this dirt.

(As an aside, I was reading the labels on the sprinklers and came across one that said: 'For outside use with cold water only.' I spent most of the rest of the day trying to imagine the lawsuit that prompted *that* warning. Most of the scenarios I envisioned involved someone named "JoeBob" installing a "discount shower head.")

As I was checking out, I had yet another opportunity to plumb the depths of ignorance of Home Depot employees. I had managed to find a sprinkler with a forty foot watering radius, and picked up ten of them. We're talking football field irrigation power here, people. I get to the register and the cashier asks me what project I'm working on.

"Well," I say, "I have this huge area that I don't know what to do with, so I figure I'll put in grass."

"Oh," she says, ringing up the ten-pack of industrial strength sprinklers, each of which can water over three thousand square feet. "Or you could build a shed."

A shed. A *shed*. Yes! Why didn't I think of that? A *twenty thousand square foot shed!* I'd put the gardening implements and potting soil in one corner, and play arena football and store small aircraft in the rest of it! Brilliant!

I suppose it's a good thing that jobs at Home Depot are available for such people, because I'm pretty sure she'd be a ward of the state otherwise. Of course, she's about two years away from being replaced by a self-checkout lane, so I hope she's saving her money.

And not only do they not know anything about what they're selling; you can't even get a dumb look from these people because they have been conditioned from day one to avoid eye contact with anyone who isn't also wearing an orange apron.

You know what I'm talking about. It's how I used to get free meals at the cafeteria in college. While all the sheep are waiting in line, meal cards in hand, you stride boldly past, your eyes affixed on something in the distance. Your body language says, "I am supposed to be over THERE. Not *here*. *Here* does not concern me. The only thing that matters is that I get over THERE, as quickly as possible." And the nice old lady or Canadian sliding cards through the scanner lets you past without raising an eyebrow, because it's pretty clear from the way you're striding boldly and actively ignoring her that you have serious business to attend to in THERE, and even if you don't, she's a food service worker getting minimum wage for sliding plastic cards through a slot, not the friggin' Secret Service.

Slowe Despot employees (see what I did there?) have made the Walk of Purposefulness into an art form. These people must train by running a gauntlet of customers trying to flag them down.

"What did Billy do wrong, people?"

"He made eye contact."

"And...?"

"He asked if they needed help."

"What should he have said?"

"'This isn't my department.'"

"Very good. We also would have accepted, 'Let me see if I can find someone to help you,' or 'I'm on my break.'"

I thought about comparison of the relative merits of the employees of each of the home improvement mammoths, but that would probably be about as interesting as a cricket match between Hellen Keller and Jabba the Hutt. So I decided to do a comparison between a typical home improvement store employee and an inanimate object. Shopping cars, in particular.

Shopping Carts vs. Home Improvement Store Employees

Availability

Unless you're shopping at 10 am on the Saturday before the 4th of July, the odds are that you're going to find a cart. Maybe not one of the big heavy lumber carts, but hey, it's not going to kill the kids to get a little exercise this time.

In contrast, unless you've got a taser gun, your odds of bagging an employee are far worse. And again, even if you do have a taser gun, the odds of getting one of the big heavy ones are pretty poor.

Winner: Carts.

Appearance

At older stores, many of the carts are pretty beat up. Still, they generally retain their overall pleasant orangey appearance.

Even at newer stores, the employees are pretty beat up, and have long since lost any orangey demeanor.

Winner: Carts.

Subject Matter Knowledge

The carts don't know much except how to go straight, and some of them can't even manage that.

Most employees can walk straight and answer simple questions in their area of expertise, be it TomKat, Brangelina or their stupid jerk boss who won't give them next Thursday off.

Winner: Employees.

Politeness

Both carts and employees tend to ignore you until you give them a little shove. The cart will then respond by moving a little in the direction you shoved it. The employee will generally glare at you and possibly shove back.

Winner: Carts.

Intangibles

Defective carts and employees both sometimes making whiny or rubby noises as they move. Often a cart will offer you a brochure of expired coupons and a half-empty cup of Mountain Dew. Often an employee will offer you a "Have a nice day" when you're buying a new hot water heater at 9:45 pm on a Sunday.

Winner: Tie.

Summary

Carts, though slightly dumber than the typical employee, are the clear winner. Avoid the ones that squeak and veer unexpectedly to the left and you should be fine. The same is true for employees.

"Are You the Responsible Parent?"

Last week I built a tree house. This week my son broke his arm.

There is, in the inevitable succession of those two statements, some support for a deterministic view of the universe.

Technically I didn't build the tree house. I took the easy way out: I put a house in a tree.

Climber, my seven-year-old son, is not known for taking the easy way out. Let's say, for example, that he needed to get down from said tree house. One option would be to use the ladder. But using ladders does not earn one the name Climber.

I was grading our future driveway with the tractor when my five year old daughter, Speed Pony, ran over to me and told me that Climber fell and hurt himself. I found Climber lying in the dirt under the tree, crying. His elbow looked strangely flat, as if his forearm had been pulled out of the joint. We hopped in the car and sped to the emergency room, where we then proceeded to wait for an hour while climber moaned and cried, his forearm hanging in a sweatshirt I had tied around his neck.

It's a surreal experience, and wholly incomprehensible to a seven-year-old, to sit in a waiting room with a dislocated elbow while medical professionals meander about on the other side of the glass, drinking coffee, doing paperwork and performing other tasks that could probably wait until after all of your limbs are properly attached. I glanced around the busy waiting room, trying to locate anyone with a condition remotely as severe as Climber's. A big black guy wandered in, having hit his head. "It really hurts," he told the woman behind the desk. There was a kid in soccer getup lying on his side across two chairs. There was an overweight woman who had been wheeled in by an EMT. "Here are your medicines," the EMT said, handing her a plastic grocery bag filled with prescription bottles. A few minutes later I saw her smoking outside, and wondered if the cigarettes had been in the bag. I supposed that if it weren't for the cigarettes, the bag would have been a lot lighter.

Finally we made it in, having been deemed worthy of "prompt care." I can only imagine the kind of dilatory care that was reserved for the "It really hurts" guy. A nurse asked us insanely irrelevant questions and made Climber stand on a scale, presumably to see whether a broken arm weighs more than a regular arm. Then we waited some more.

While we were waiting, I had some time to think, which is never a good thing. It occurred to me that an emergency room is like the Bizarro universe version of a car dealership. I know, I'm insane, but stick with me. First, an emergency room is staffed with highly educated professionals who actively ignore you, whereas a car dealership is staffed with high school dropouts who eye-rape you as you step onto the lot. Second, the goal of the car dealership is to sell you something that you don't need and can't afford, *right now*, before you've had a minute to reconsider your decision, whereas the goal of the emergency room is to make you wait for six hours so you can think about whether it's really worth it to fork over a $50 copay to have a limb reattached. Third, the clientele of a car dealership tends to be made up of yuppies and wealthy retirees, whereas... well, the emergency room's isn't.

But what prompted this comparison was the realization that the doctors and nurses didn't seem to notice that I existed. Every comment and question was directed to my wife, as if I were just an unnecessary appendage dangling by a bit of cartilage. "Is he on any medications?" "How far did he fall?" "Has he had any other injuries?" I had the answers to all these questions too, but their gazes flitted between my wife and my son. I felt like raising my hand. "Me! Pick me! I know this one!" Throw me a bone here, people.

My opportunity to get my participation grade came when Mrs. Diesel left momentarily to take Speed Pony to the bathroom. A nurse began to ask me some questions, and I thought I did an admirable job of demonstrating that I was an involved parent who was only indirectly responsible for his son's deformed elbow. But I got the sense she was asking me easy questions, like you do when you're waiting for a preschooler's mommy to show up. "How old are you?" "Do you like trains?" "When did your mommy say she was going to be back?" And sure enough, as soon as Mrs. Diesel returned, I was once again banished to the realm of child beaters and vestigial appendages. "Were there any men in the vicinity who could have yanked the arm right out of the socket at the time of the injury?" they asked my wife, who nodded knowingly. I went to get some coffee.

I took Speed Pony to Grandma's, and by the time I got back, Climber's arm was in a sling and he was coming out of sedation. "I was sleeping," he complained through a drug-induced haze as the nurses poked and prodded at him. When they finally left him alone, he told us that he had been dreaming about some third graders who were pushing him around.

Apparently they had popped his arm back into place (that would give me nightmares about bullying third graders too!), and all was well except for a chip of bone that had broken off the tip of his elbow. This required an MRI, and depending on the outcome of that, may require surgery. I'm 29 years older than Climber and I've never had an MRI or surgery. I've never even broken a bone. I feel like I've been cheated out of some defining experiences in my life, and I'm not just saying that because my seven year old has tried morphine and I never even got drunk on Natural Light until I was 17.

Anyway, Climber is now wearing a cast and in no apparent pain. We'll see in the next few days what additional treatment, if any, he needs. The other day I caught him trying to climb up to the tree house, so I guess it's safe to say he's not experiencing any serious psychological trauma.

Aloha! And Good Riddance!

Over the course of our fourteen years of marriage, Mrs. Diesel and I have stayed in some scary motels. Being of Dutch stock, we're unnaturally frugal, and even now that we could probably afford to shell out an extra $40 for a Best Western, it's sort of a demented game we play, trying to find the cheapest imaginable motel in a given area.

We stayed in a several crummy motels during our ten-day trek from Michigan to California eleven years ago (some day I'll blog about that nightmare journey. Suffice to say it took us ten days, three of which were spent in Rapid City, South Dakota). After paying for a room at one place that had delusions of respectability, the clerk noticed that our luggage included a large plastic case with air holes in it. Luther, our big black cat, was traveling with us. "We don't allow cats," she said.

"Well, we've already paid for the room, and we can't leave him in the car." I said.

After some grumbling, she said we could have the cat in the room. "But don't let him sleep on the bed," she said.

We spent the night watching TV in bed, with Luther between us. Whenever he would close his eyes, we'd snap, "Hey, wake up! No sleeping on the bed!"

In Reno, we once stayed at a motel that was on top of a convenience store. It was $15 cheaper than the second crummiest motel in town. Then there was the place in Yreka, California with the mismatched bedspreads that clashed with the garish orange wallpaper which, in turn, clashed with the red shag carpet. The surreal climax was when we opened the closet door and found a hidden stash of volleyball trophies. Just go ahead and try to envision a scenario in which six volleyball trophies end up in the closet of a motel room. I'll meet you in the next paragraph when you get back.

Astoundingly, despite this string of brushes with the low end of the hospitality industry, our worst motel experience occurred just a few days ago, on our way back from Michigan. We were scheduled to fly out of Chicago's Midway airport at 7:30am, so we drove to Chicago the night before. We pulled in at a suitably crummy motel called the Aloha – presumably because for any sane person pulling into this place, hello would also be goodbye. If there was a Hawaiian theme, I didn't notice – unless the toilets in Hawaii make a horrific screeching sound that sounds like a hippopotamus gasping for air through a saxophone.

Of course we didn't know about the screeching hippo at first. Our first sign that something was wrong – other than the fact that the motel had a sign advertising 4 hour "naps" for $20 – was when we opened the door to our room and flipped on the light switch, and no lights came on. This was probably a blessing, because what we could see by the light in the bathroom was not encouraging. I support the hiring of handicapped people as much as the next guy, but blind retarded people really shouldn't be cleaning motel bathrooms.

Next I tried turning on the TV. That didn't work either, indicating that maybe a circuit breaker had been tripped. Wires dangled from the smoke alarm, unconnected to a battery – always a good thing in a room that has electrical problems.

Fortunately the toilet did work – though at the age of 37 I'm no longer so proud of doing my business that I need the toilet to announce it to the folks six doors down from us. Seriously, it was that loud. I don't know what you have to do to a toilet to cause it to make that noise, but it can't be healthy for either the perpetrator or the toilet.

Ya think?

My parents ran a motel for ten years, so I know better than to touch a motel bedspread without a hazmat suit, but the sheets at least looked clean. Even the yellow marks around the cigarette burns had been bleached almost white. And really, clean sheets are all I require in a motel room. Well, clean sheets, working lights, a TV and a toilet that isn't possessed by evil spirits.

I went to the office to ask if we could get a different room. The clerk was a young woman of Iranipakafghanindian descent, so she had a hard time understanding what my problem was. It wasn't until I managed to communicate, through a variety of complex gesticulations, that our toilet was possessed by Flushscreemi, the Iranipakafghanindian goddess of the maelstrom, that she agreed to have the maintenance guy come and "fix all of the problems." Five minutes, she said.

Ten minutes later we were still in our room, entertaining ourselves by not watching TV in the dark. I headed back to the office and told the kids to come with me. "We're going to play a game," I said. "It's called 'Make as Much Noise as You Can.'" The kids happily complied by yelling back and forth to each other in the lobby until the maintenance guy showed up.

After twenty minutes of the maintenance guy calling us periodically on the phone to ask us whether the lights were working yet, we were finally offered another room. The alternate room was right next to the lobby, which would have been a drawback if we could have heard anything over the roar of the traffic. There was no problem with the TV in this room, because there was no TV in this room. One of the two lights worked, and we were blessedly free of the tormented wails of Flushscreemi. A massive crack running down the bathroom mirror had been repaired with what looked like strawberry yogurt. We had the maintenance guy move the TV from the other room, not so much because we wanted to watch TV as because we wanted to watch him carry a TV down a flight of stairs.

But other than a few games of Make as Much Noise as You Can played in the lobby by participants of varying skill levels over the next several hours, and the incessant chirping of a smoke alarm that refused to go quietly into that good night, our stay was relatively undisturbed. And when it comes down to it, all you really need in a motel is clean sheets and a comfortable bed. And at least one light. And a non-screeching toilet. And maybe some twine to tie up the seven year old in bed next to you who seems to be dreaming about falling from trees.

I looked forward to getting some sleep on the plane.

3

Driving

In which the author tries desperately to convince his readers that he's just a "regular guy."

Someone once asked me whether I believed in the theory of intelligent design. It's a compelling idea, but as someone who has driven back and forth between my home and San Francisco Bay area over a thousand times, I'm not even sure there's an intelligent entity guiding the construction of the California highway system.

For most of the past eleven years, I drove from the Central Valley to the San Francisco Bay Area three to four days a week. Like most Americans, I love driving my car. Unfortunately I found that a large percentage of these Americans were in front of me on I-580 on any given day, driving six miles an hour as they drive past a stalled Chevy Cavalier on the shoulder. It's a Chevy Cavalier, people. Stalling is what they *do*. If you see one running you have my permission to gawk. Now get out of the $#%*ing way!

The upside, in addition to learning useful Spanish phrases like *Somos todos medicos aqui* ("We're all doctors here") from my Learn to Speak Spanish CDs, is that I had a lot of time to think – and a lot of time to observe people doing stupid things in, around, and to their cars. Sometimes I'd be so busy laughing at all the morons on the road that I'd be three exits past the office before I realized where I was. Which wouldn't be so bad, except that it was Saturday, and I was supposed to be going to Target for cat food.

I don't commute any more, for the simple reason that I have no job to commute to. Traffic was a major factor in making the decision to scrap the whole working-for-money-that-can-be-exchanged-for-goods-and-services idea. Over the years that I commuted, I saw the traffic go from ridiculous to absolutely insane. It got so bad toward the end that I routinely exited the freeway to take a shortcut through the Pleasanton mall parking lot to avoid the inevitable traffic snarl. Now I'm no civil engineer, but I know that something is wrong when the shortest route between two cities entails cutting through Best Buy.

When you think about it, our whole driving culture is a little bizarre. I mean, we give driver's licenses to sixteen year boys. These are kids who can't be trusted to wear pants properly, and we're letting them operate two-thousand pound machines that can travel a hundred miles an hour. Somehow we as a society have concluded that virtually anyone over 15 who isn't legally blind or paralyzed is qualified to drive a Lincoln Navigator past a preschool in a snowstorm. We gasp at a twenty-eight car pileup on the freeway, but what is really amazing is that these occurrences are actually quite rare. Despite the fact that a solid majority of us are completely out of our depth operating anything more complicated than an electric can opener, most of the time most of us avoid doing anything that would get us or someone else killed.

I, for example, know almost nothing about how my car works. Oh, I could tell you how, in theory, an internal combustion engine works, just like I could tell you how, in theory, I will some day be eligible to collect Social Security. I'm pretty sure both of these systems involve a large wheel and several hungry squirrels, but I'm hazy on the details.

Needless to say, our surreal driving culture makes for good comic fodder. I could write an entire book about the idiotic things people do when driving. See, here's a perfect example: Some guy in front of me has had his turn signal on the whole time I've been writing this. Idiot.

WTF?

I can't prove it, but I swear I drove by a truck this morning that had the letters WTF plastered along its side. There was some more lettering about whatever business the truck was in, and maybe a phone number, but all I had time to make out was WTF. Which is, coincidentally, what I was thinking when I saw it.

I mean, WTF? What kind of name is that? I spent most of the day wondering what kind of business WTF might be in. I imagined that maybe they deliver expensive and bizarre novelty gifts, like a grand piano made entirely out of cheese ("this C sharp cheddar is delicious!") or dead farm animals stuffed with potpourri. I can see the commercials now: A woman looks out the kitchen window to see two men unloading a large stuffed goat, and says, "Honey, WTF is in the driveway?" And her husband says, "Yes they are! Happy anniversary, dear. And thanks, WTF!"

I tried to take a picture of the WTF truck with my camera phone, but my timing was a bit off so I ended up with a picture of my dashboard and part of my steering wheel, which actually isn't as interesting as it sounds. Come to think of it, this raises an intriguing question. In California they are making it illegal to use a cell phone while driving. But does that mean it's going to be illegal to take pictures with your cell phone camera while driving as well? I hope not. I rely on my camera phone to document all the interesting stuff I see while I'm driving, like my dashboard and part of my steering wheel.

Artist's Rending of WTF Truck

I'd like to be the test case for that no-cell-phone-while-driving law. I imagine the courtroom exchange going something like this:

> **Diesel:** Your honor, I wasn't using my phone while driving, and I can prove it. These pictures clearly demonstrate that I could not possibly have been talking on the phone when Officer Fredericks pulled me over, because I was too busy taking pictures with it.
>
> **Judge:** Well, let's see them.
>
> **Diesel:** Ok, this is a hot jogger chick I drove past shortly before Officer Fredericks pulled me over. See, she's giving me the finger.
>
> **Judge:** Uh huh.

Diesel: And this is Officer Frederick's flashers in my rear view mirror.

Judge: Ok...

Diesel: And here's Officer Fredericks, walking up to my car. See how mean he looks?

Judge: Hmm...

Diesel: Here he is again, closer up. See?

Judge: He does look kind of mean.

Diesel: That's what I'm saying. This is his hand, trying to grab my cell phone.

Judge: What's this next one?

Diesel: That's my dashboard, and part of my steering wheel.

Judge: Nice composition.

Diesel: Thanks.

Judge: What about this one?

Diesel: Oh, that's a couple of guys unloading a Virgin Mary shrine made from pancakes and old Spice Girls CDs.

Judge: WTF?

Diesel: Of course!

Judge: Well, I have no choice but to find you not guilty.

Diesel: Hey, that's great! And thanks, WTF!

State of Anxiety

A few weeks ago my family took a road trip from our home in northern California to a resort in Colorado for a family reunion for my mom's side of the family (count the prepositional phrases in that sentence and win a puppy!). I informed a friend about the upcoming trip, adding that my mom's family was "crazy big." She responded, "You mean they're crazy? Or they're really tall? Or the family is really big?"

I replied, "Yes."

She thought for a second, and then said, "So it's like a Special Olympics basketball camp?"

Which is an uncanny description of what these reunions are actually like. Except there's no basketball.

To get to Colorado from northern California you have to go through Nevada, Utah, and Wyoming. The kids loved the scenery: the cacti, the rocky cliffs, the desert plateaus.... And that crazy coyote! Man, they must have watched that DVD like 16 times.

Look, I'm sorry. California is beautiful, and Colorado is pretty cool, but I can't figure out why God stuck all that dirt in between them. Nevada has its attractions, but they're mostly immoral, and frankly too expensive. Utah is what Nevada would be if it were run by Mormons. And Wyoming is what Utah would be if all the Mormons left.

I have to say, though, that they all have better roads than California. If you've ever driven into California on I-80 you know what I'm talking about. You'll be zipping along toward Tahoe, exhilarating in the sight of mountains and redwoods after 16 hours of scrub-covered sand, and it occurs to you that you should slow down and get into the right lane so you can take it all in. But then you realize that there's an 18 inch altitude differential between lanes, and that it's going to take every ounce of skill and concentration that you possess not to end up in the Truckee River. Potholes start flying at you like asteroids at the Millennium

Falcon, and woodland creatures dart in front of you like furry little suicide bombers. All the while, insane California drivers are flying past at ridiculous speeds, usually while talking on a cell phone, drinking a latte, and knitting a poncho from hemp fibers. By the time you get to Sacramento, you need to check yourself into a facility to be treated for PTSD.

Utah, on the other hand, has fantastic roads. There were crews of Mormons resurfacing highways in Utah that looked like they were still wet from the last time they were resurfaced. (The highways, that is, not the Mormons.) The roads had so many layers of fresh asphalt that the locals gave directions by saying, "First, get on top of the road...." And these are highways that are built over the salt flats, which are used for by auto manufacturers to test cars. That's right, they are resurfacing roads that are built on top of the world's largest parking lot. I don't know why they don't just send a guy out to run across the desert with a can of spray paint so they can spend their highway funds on booze and cigarettes.

Oh well, I guess we all have our own vices. Even the Golden State has its faults.

Failure to Appear

As a person who has no job, no schedule, and very few commitments of any kind, it's essential that I drive ridiculously fast so as not to waste any of the 11 waking hours at my disposal on any given day. I average around 40 miles per hour, but that number goes up considerably if I'm out for more than 20 minutes.

I live on a dead end road, so to go anywhere I have to first get on a road charmingly called I-99 Frontage. The speed limit on this road is 40 miles per hour, which I take to mean that I should drive no more than 40 miles per hour faster than the traffic on the highway next to me. After all, Einstein proved that all motion is relative, so who's to say how fast I'm "really" driving? And of course Heisenberg demonstrated that you can't know where you are and how fast you're traveling at the same time, which means that any cop who has pinpointed my velocity doesn't have a chance in hell of catching me.

I tried to explain this to the cop who pulled me over a few months ago. "Do you know how fast you were driving?" he asked. "No," I said cheerfully, "But I know exactly where I am!"[*]

He was kind enough not to ticket me for speeding, letting me off with a stern lecture about blind corners, stopping distances, and – I think – something about the Romulan neutral zone. Thank God they don't test you for ADD when they give you your driver's license. Anyway, he did that cop thing where they find some innocuous offense to give you a ticket for that you didn't even know was illegal, because they feel sorry for you and don't really feel like hauling your ass to jail for attempting to outrace the earth's rotation. They might, for example, give you a ticket for driving under the influence of 18th century romantic poetry, or having one eyelash too few. In my case, I got a "repair and report" ticket for not having a front license plate.

(Aside: Who knew you even needed a front license plate? I thought the front license plate was an optional thing, like voting or registering for Selective Service.)

In point of fact, I did have a front license plate. It was in the back of my car, under the carpet and a pile of 4" ABS pipe fittings, where admittedly it would be difficult to see from a distance. I didn't tell the nice cop about this because (1) I didn't want him to have to ticket me for something more egregious, such as Misuse of General Relativity for Personal Gain (I believe that's a "one-eight-niner" in police lingo); and (2) I had forgotten it was there.

I was given 30 days to "repair" the problem and "report" to the proper authorities. It took me roughly 29 days to repair the problem, the "repair" process consisting of the following steps:

---

[*] I didn't actually say this. In fact, I didn't even make up this joke. It may seem odd to steal a joke that virtually no one will get, but isn't that the kind of shiftless irrationality that makes one truly original?

71

Days 1-21	Denial
Day 22	"Where the hell is that license plate? Hey, I bet it's still in the back of my car!"
Days 23-25	Procrastination
Day 26	Attach license plate
Day 27-28	Procrastination
Day 29	Go to police station to have a cop sign the ticket

So you can see, I just made it under the wire. Then, unfortunately, I spent another 68 days in denial about the "report" part, which would have consisted of simply showing up at the court office to display the newly autographed ticket. During this period various "courtesy" notices began arriving in the mail, courteously informing me of the myriad fees, fines, levies and dams (as in, "dam, that's a big levy") that had been added to the original ticket amount of $10. Warren Buffet couldn't have turned $10 into $425 that fast. The main thing that had been added was a "Failure to Appear" charge, which makes it sound like there was a courtroom full of people with nothing to do but twiddle their thumbs while they anxiously awaited for me to show up. "What time did he say he would be here?" they fret. "Should we call?"

So finally I went to the court office to pay the fines. A lady in a forest green blouse sat behind the window. As I began to explain my situation, she stood up and another woman in what appeared to be exactly the same blouse took her place. "We're switching," said the second woman.

"Ok, well you're wearing the same shirt, so this should be an easy transition," I said.

I got the feeling that I wasn't the first one to point this out to them that day. Note to self: Do not immediately alienate someone who may have discretion over whether you have to pay several hundred dollars in fines.

I showed them my "courtesy notice" and there was some discussion about whether they could reduce the amount or not. It turned out that they could not, but I had the option of going to court to get the amount reduced. It sounded like all you had to do was show up and you were pretty much guaranteed to get the amount knocked down quite a bit. Evidently Woody Allen was right: 90% of life is just showing up. I thought for a moment. "How long does that usually take?" I asked. Because again, I'm a busy, busy man. Places to go, things to do. I can't be sitting around for 2 hours just to save a few hundred bucks.

I was assured that it usually went quite fast. So I said ok, and they said that I needed to show up at 8:30 next Wednesday to put my name on the list for the afternoon. I didn't ask why I couldn't just put my name on the list now, as it presumably had something to do with the fact that persons of my unsavory character couldn't be trusted to keep an appointment without being forced to physically drag our asses down there first thing in the morning to demonstrate that we were still alive and reasonably sober.

"At the very least, you should be able to clear up that Failure to Appear," said Ms. Greenshirt. Yes, I thought. One might think I had cleared it up already by in fact *appearing*. Whatever. I didn't mind appearing again. I'm pretty good at appearing. Sometimes I appear seven or eight times a day without even knowing it. I can even appear drunk or hung-over if I need to. I believe that sort of thing is generally frowned upon in the courtroom, though, so I resolved to appear sober.

I showed up that Wednesday at 8:30 am, went home for 4 hours (during which time I admirably remained almost completely sober), then turned around and drove back to the courthouse. As I entered, I was promptly examined by a swarthy security guard with a thick accent who was wearing a turban and had a beard down to his waist. I decided, in a remarkable display of high-mindedness, not to find this the least bit ironic.

While I waited in line I noticed a sign that had been pasted to the wall. It read:

No Shoes
No Shirt
No Tanktops
No Court

I considered asking how many tank tops I was expected to bring into court; whether I was supposed to wear them or carry them in a bag; if the judge had a color preference; etc., but decided against it. Again, do not aggravate people who know a lot of people who carry guns, no matter how confused their signs are.

The actual court proceedings were rather uninteresting. It was an awful lot like *Night Court*, actually, except that it wasn't night, and the judge didn't do any magic tricks. Surprisingly, though, Mel Torme did show up for a cameo.

The judge eventually called my name, and I pretended I didn't know English. "Nolo contendre," I said, and the judge smiled and told me that he would knock the fine down to $110 bucks. I could hardly believe my ruse had worked. Silly judge, I thought. I've got this guy wrapped around my *habeas corpus*.

It turns out that $110 actually means $130 in government dollars. Seriously. California passed a law after 9/11 legislating that any fine is actually $20 more than it is. They didn't actually increase the fines; they just said, "Whatever your fine is, it's still that same amount. Oh, and give us another $20 for, um, security." Because when you steal $20 from millions of Californians, you need a lot of security.

So then I got to wait in line again, this time to hand them my check for One Hundred Ten Dollars and 2000/100ths. While I waited at the Traffic Offenses window, various low-lifes and victims of low-lifes came and went at the Miscellaneous Grievances window (It may not actually have been called that). One guy seemed to be tagging along with a friend of his, who was involved in some kind of domestic dispute. Either he had requested a restraining order against someone, or someone had requested a restraining order against him, or he and someone had filed a mutual restraining order against each other, or something along those lines. Anyway, when the guy was done, his friend walked up to the window and said, "Can I get one of those?"

This surprised me, as I had never thought of a restraining order as an impulse purchase. Apparently the clerk had made it sound so appealing that this guy had been sold on the concept. Well, almost sold. "Do I have to fill out all those papers?" he said. Rule of thumb: If ten minutes of paperwork is too much of a hurdle for you to get a restraining order, you may want to reconsider whether a restraining order is really the right choice for you. Maybe you'd be interested in our Change Your Phone Number and Stop Wasting Tax Dollars on Your Domestic Squabbles program?

I paid my fines, so I'm back in the good graces of the state of California. I'm sure they're happy, because now that I have both license plates on my car, they can literally get me coming and going. Actually, now that I think about it, if I had had both license plates when the cop pulled me over, I probably would have gotten a huge speeding ticket, since he wouldn't have had the option of giving me the license plate ticket instead. I should probably take that front one off again, just in case. Maybe I'll get to it tomorrow.

All in all, it wasn't such a bad experience, although it did take up a few hours of my day. I drove like a madman all the way home. Places to go, things to do.

Just Give Me a Sign

I have a confession to make. Most of the stuff on my MySpace profile is lies. I wasn't really born on another planet, those aren't my favorite TV shows, and the movies I listed were selected purely for their metallurgical properties. I really am a Taurus, though, which explains all the bullshit.

I debated whether I should display my zodiacal sign, because I don't really buy into that stuff (Tauruses as a rule are skeptical about astrology). In my case the profile does fit, though: I'm stubborn and opinionated, and I spend a lot of time charging full speed at colorful objects that are dangled in front of me only to be jerked away at the last second. I don't make a lot of major decisions based on my horoscope, although I did buy a Ford Taurus once, which turned out to be a big mistake. So was my Ford Bronco II. Ford loves naming vehicles after temperamental animals. Maybe if they came out with the Ford Labrador, people would start buying their cars again.

There definitely should be more cars named after signs of the zodiac. (There was the Dodge Aries, of course, but that name was wasted on a car that Chrysler, in a moment of marketing genius, had already named after the letter K.) I know I would jump at the chance to own a Toyota Sagittarius or an Oldsmobile Cancer. Actually, GM doesn't make Oldsmobiles any more, do they? I wonder why not. Most companies would kill for a brand that suggests the product is outdated as soon as it's rolled off the assembly line. As if to indicate that the division was in on its last legs, in the mid-80s GM came out with the Oldsmobile Omega, the most ominous sounding car name since the AMC Death Knell.

I don't actually know anything about cars, of course, and like most people I fill the gap in my knowledge with fear and superstition. This is why automobiles and astrology are such a perfect fit. Why stand on the side of the road with your hood up acting like you're trying to figure out if the fetzer valve is properly connected to the flux capacitor, when you could just blame the problem on the alignment of the planets and wait for a tow truck? Speaking of which, I should go call my mechanic, because my Saturn is in retrograde again.

The California Driver Test

Think you have what it takes to navigate California's roadways? That's ok, none of the other drivers do either.

1. When moving to the left lane from the center lane on an interstate highway, you should:

a) Match the speed of the traffic in the left lane and then move over when you see an opening.

b) Turn on your left turn signal and wait for the drivers to your left to make room for you.

c) Try to make eye contact with a driver in the left lane and communicate using crude sign language that you want to get over.

d) Tap your brakes and turn on your right turn signal. Drift slightly to the right and then veer sharply to the left while gunning the gas and honking your horn. Assume other drivers will move.

2. The use of exit numbers on interstate highways became mandatory in 1971. When did California begin implementing exit numbers interstates?

a) 1968

b) 1971

c) 2002

d) 1973

3. A 4 lane highway where traffic slows to a crawl every weekday at 3:30 in the afternoon:

a) Should be widened as soon as possible.

b) Is a good rationale for more public transportation.

c) Is a good argument for a coordinated plan to prevent sprawl.

d) Is a good place for an exit for a new housing development.

4. The phrase "RIGHT LANE EXIT ONLY" means:

a) If you are in the right lane, you must exit the freeway.

b) If you are in the right lane and do not want to exit the freeway, you must merge left as soon as possible.

c) If you are exiting the freeway, you must be in the right lane.

d) If you want to zip past 200 pathetic rule-obeying saps, here's your chance.

5. A stretch of asphalt that has massive potholes about every 100 feet:

a) Should be closed for repairs immediately.

b) Is justification for another 11/32 of a cent sales tax.

c) Is an indication that the state is squandering its federal highway funds.

d) Must be some sort of runway.

6. Draw a line indicating the best driving route between point A and point B:

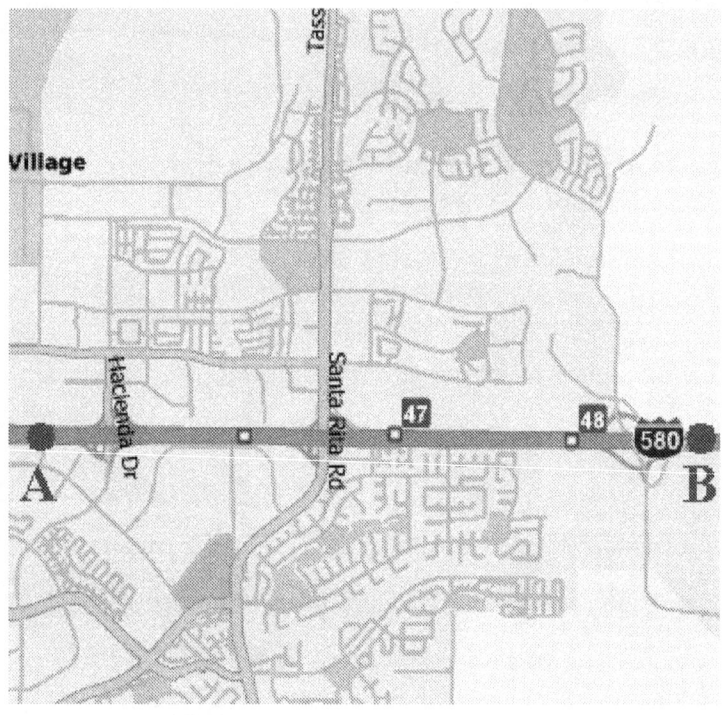

7. If the roadway is wet, you should:

a) Drive slightly slower and more carefully than usual, because water can make the road slippery.

b) Drive the same speed as usual, because your boss doesn't care that the road is wet, you still have to be at work by 8.

c) Drive WAY slower than normal, because water falling out of the sky is an omen of some kind of impeding disaster.

d) Drive WAY faster than normal, because hydroplaning is the most fun you can have with your clothes on.

e) Any of the above except (a).

8. In 2004 California voters passed a $3 billion bond proposition to:

a) Retrofit bridges and tunnels for earthquake protection.

b) Fund public transportation projects.

c) Build several new state highways.

d) Research ways to clone more people.

ANSWERS:

1. d

2. c

3. d

4. d

5. d

6. (See below)

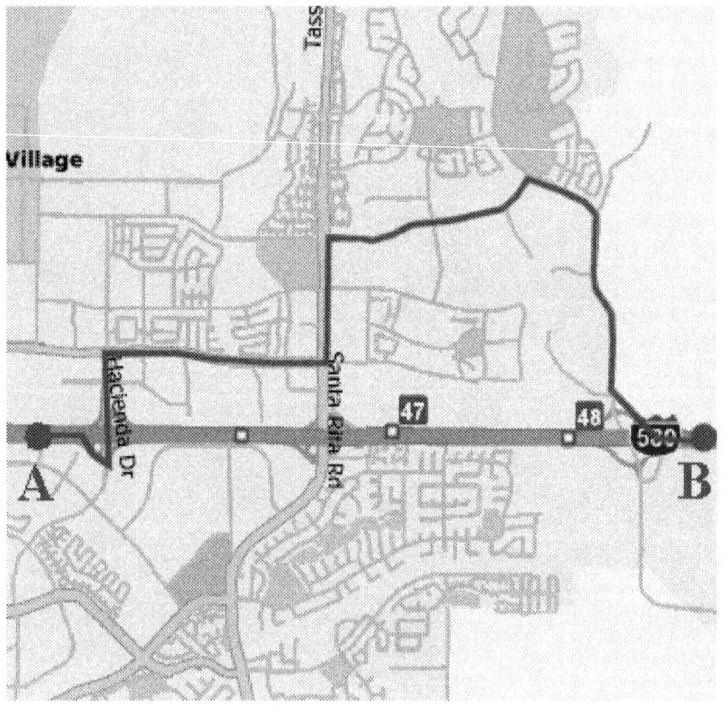

7. e

8. d

SCORING

0-1 Don't move. We'll come get you.

2-3 You should probably stick to side streets. And don't leave Nebraska.

4-5 You may be able to drive on California's highways for short periods of time without experiencing any severe trauma.

6-7 You are a born California commuter! Your cell phone and handgun are on the way.

8 I hear Cal Trans is looking for a new director.

Perpetual Motion

I once worked with a guy who claimed to have invented a perpetual motion machine. He didn't call it a perpetual motion machine, of course. I think he called it a "self-powered car." As I recall, the car worked like this:

- A laser heats a container of water to boiling.
- The pressure from the steam makes the car's wheels turn.
- A generator hooked up to the car's wheels makes electricity.
- The electricity powers the laser.

I think there were 3 or 4 more steps in there somewhere which would have dispersed any energy that actually made it from step one to step four, but you get the idea. Not only was the car impossible; it was impossible in an almost unbelievably stupid way. Did he think that the engineers at GM were just waiting for the moment when someone would whisper into their ears the magical words *laser-powered steam turbine*? "Eureka!" they would shout. "If only we had thought to combine 19th century technology with untempered ignorance!"

"That's called a perpetual motion machine," I told him. "It's impossible. You lose energy at every step of the system. Hell, you'd probably lose 95%

of the energy you started out with on the steam conversion alone." *Not to mention 100% of your credibility*, I thought.

"It's not a perpetual motion machine," he said. "If you brake, the car will stop, and then you'd need more energy to get it started again. That's why there's a battery." *Ah, another step. More energy loss. Good thinking.*

"Ok," I said. "So you have a tank of water, right? And you heat the water. Now let's say you put your hand near the tank. Will it feel warm?"

"Of course."

"Right. That's heat. Heat is energy. You're losing energy from the system in the form of radiated heat."

"No, the heat boils the water. You're not losing it."

I think I argued with him for about two hours before I gave up. I also once had a debate with him about faith versus science. He fancied himself an atheist, and scoffed at me for believing things that couldn't be proved.

"What do you believe in?" I asked.

"Science."

"And what is science based on?"

"Experiments."

"And how do people observe experiments?"

"Uhhh..."

"With our senses, right. And how do you know that what your senses tell you is true?"

"Uhhh..."

A perpetual motion machine that is far too simple to work.

"Experience, right. Because your senses have been reliable in the past. But how do you know that what you experience with your senses isn't all just one big illusion. How do you know that you're not just a brain in a vat?"

"Uhhh..."

"You don't, right. At some point you just have to make a leap of faith. I make a leap of faith by believing in God, and you make one by believing in science. It just takes a few more step to get to yours."

"So science is still better."

"Whaaa...?"

"It has more steps."

More steps. That was his answer. Make the system complicated enough that you can't see that it's all bullshit. Hey, it worked for the self-powered car, right?

Still, his car was pretty simple. Anyone with a 4th grade education could have understood (and probably designed) it. I suggested he needed more steps to further complicate it, thus shielding the car further from reality. Something like:

- A garden grows on top of the car.
- A dinosaur eats from the garden.
- The dinosaur dies, turning into fertilizer for the garden and fossil fuels.
- The members of the Coal workers Local 327, who live in the glove compartment, come out and mine the coal when it's ready, loading it into a furnace.
- The furnace burns the coal, heating a container of water, which turns into steam.
- The steam turns a turbine which drives a generator, which powers a laser.
- The laser heats another container of water almost to boiling.
- The water is shot through finely ground coffee, in order to make espresso.
- The driver sips the espresso while waiting patiently for a tow truck.

Hey, GM has done dumber stuff. If this idea takes off, maybe Daimler will buy them. Then there will be no stopping them! I mean, unless they hit the brakes.

Don't Try This When Not at Home

The other day as I was driving to work I happened to look over at the guy driving in the lane next to me and noticed that he was reading a magazine. Not checking a map, not glancing at an ad for male enhancement products, actually *reading* a magazine while he was driving. He had it propped up on his steering wheel as if the manufacturer had intended it to be used as a handy reading stand. It makes you wonder why they don't put a little clip on the top of the steering wheel for holding your reading material, and maybe a little lamp in case it gets too dark to see clearly. I guess carmakers figure there's enough interesting stuff going on in the windshield and mirrors to keep your attention. It must take a serious case of ADD to be so bored with the imminent possibility of a ten car pile-up that you have to spice things up by perusing a magazine while hurtling down I-5. I hope it was *Dismemberment and Disfigurement Monthly*, because otherwise he's going to have some catching up to do when he gets out of the coma.

Despite the fact that everybody knows how stupid it is to drink and drive or to grab a downed power line with your bare hands, they still have public service announcements telling you not to do those things. Yet there are no PSAs warning against reading and driving. This prompts the question: How reckless and dangerous does something have to be for no one to have even thought of warning you not to do it? Congratulations, Bob, you've just vaulted into a completely new demographic of stupidity! It never even occurred to us to warn people not to do that. We'll add it to the list of future PSAs, right under "Don't stick Legos up your nose" and "Don't throw rocks at mountain lions."

I've even heard of people getting ticketed for watching TV while driving. I bet this happens more than you might think. And given all the niche cable networks that exist today, I imagine that the TV-watching driver demographic is probably large enough to support their own network. The Driver Network would be a big hit. They could play *The Cannonball Run, Knight Rider*, and all the latest police chases. And every once in a while they'd break in with a public service announcement that says, "Watch the road, you moron!"

4

Culture, Pop and Otherwise

In which the author continues to use self-deprecation to make himself feel better about attacking people who never did anything to him.

What a stupid title for a chapter. I was going to call it "Pop Culture," but I'm not sure I understand what pop culture is. Pop culture must be to culture what pop music is to music. Or maybe what pop rocks are to rocks. Whatever it is, you shouldn't mix it with soda or you'll end up like that kid Mikey from the Life cereal commercials. Do you know what happened to him? Me neither. Weird, huh? He just *disappeared*. Creepy.

So this chapter is all about the peculiarities of American culture that I find simultaneously baffling and amusing. Don't get me wrong; I love the United States. In fact, often it's our unique and generally admirable qualities that result in unexpectedly bizarre behavior and surreal cultural artifacts. America is characterized by a peculiar kind of moral clarity – the kind of clarity that comes from being able to turn the earth into a radioactive slag heap eighteen times over before the rest of the world can get its pants on.

Only America could invent a character like Superman, who combines the wholesomeness and idealism of America's puritan founders with the unfathomable firepower of the nuclear age. Superman is America as we see ourselves: a nice guy, sure, but don't piss him off. Superman has been the inspiration for a thousand knock-offs and the subject of nearly as many spoofs, but he still stands tall as the paragon of "truth, justice and the American way." In an age of irony, the Man of Steel remains untarnished.

In the same way, only America could give the world *Star Wars*. Sure, George Lucas borrows indiscriminately from eastern philosophy and ancient mythology, but the idea that the world's cultures comprise one gigantic all-you-can-eat buffet is an American one. We take want we want, and leave the rest. And in the end, the force isn't about enlightenment or attaining oneness with the universe; it's about moving shit with your mind and kicking ass. In *Star Wars* the good guy wears white and the bad guy wears so much black that he had to be seven feet tall just to fit it all. There is no moral ambiguity in Star Wars, and even more importantly there's no ambiguity about the protagonist's destiny. We know Luke Skywalker is going to grow up and kick Darth Vader's ass eventually, even if he doesn't know it himself. Star Wars is the realization of the quintessentially American idea that *dammit, I'm meant for something more than hanging out in this shitty little town.*

In America, everybody is special and everybody is destined for greatness. My generation was schooled by Saturday morning cartoons telling us that each and every one of us was the "most important person in the whole wide world." We were a raised as a generation of Luke Skywalkers, free to pursue our destinies as we saw fit. And now most of us spend our days fixing moisture vaporators, only occasionally glancing up to see dim flashes of light hinting at epic struggles beyond our reach. If it weren't for the occasional trip to Tashi station to pick up power converters, we'd have no fun at all.

The Force is Middling in this One

5/30

Cam Cloudhammer, Director of Human Resources, Order of the Jedi

Dear Mr. Cloudhammer,

As a recent graduate of the Tatooine Academy of Arts and Sciences, I was excited to hear about the opening with the Jedi Knights for an entry level Force Technician I. I have long dreamed of joining the Jedi Order and I think I will be a valuable asset to your organization.

As you can see from my enclosed resume, I graduated with a 3.2 GPA and I scored a 1242 on the Force Assessment Test. I did particularly well in Advanced Midi-Chlorianology and Pre-Imperial History. I believe I could have performed even better academically, but I worked my way through school recalibrating moisture vaporators. I think the combination of my rigorous coursework and practical experience will serve me well as a Force Technician I.

I'm available for an interview on short notice on most weekdays. I know my resume probably isn't the most impressive you will receive, but I think you'll find that I'm "good Jedi material" if you take the time to meet me in person. I thank you for your time and look forward to hearing from you.

Best Regards,

Kenny Skywalker

P.S. I forgot to mention that I can type 40 words per minute and levitate small objects with my mind.

P.P.S. Not to name-drop, but in case you're wondering, Luke is my second cousin.

6/21

Heinous Vlaak, Personnel Director, Order of the Sith

Dear Mr. Vlaak,

I recently graduated from the Tatooine Academy of Arts and Sciences and was interested to learn of the part time Tractor Field Operator position that was recently posted on the Sith website. I have long been intrigued by the shadowy workings of the Sith, and have recently begun to consider a career in the service of the Empire.

As my enclosed resume indicates, I am an above average student, but I think that the highly structured nature of the Tatooine Academy prevented me from reaching my true potential, as I am something of an "outside the box" thinker. It's true that my experience with the Dark Side is limited, but my current job at the Mos Eisley Spaceport Cantina requires that I be very assertive with droids and others whose kind we don't serve. I am also led to believe that my destiny lies with the Dark Side by my co-workers' frequent reminders that I'm "really not a people person."

I thank you for your time and look forward to hearing from you.

In Your Service,

Kenneth Skywalker (No relation)

P.S. I once pantsed a Jawa, which is considered pretty evil around here. I am also good with Excel.

7/29

Boba Fett, Proprietor, Fett Investigations, Bounty Hunter and Polygraph Service

Dear Mr. Fett,

Boy, are you hard to track down! I got your contact information from a mutual acquaintance who indicated that you may have an opening for a henchmen/tough. I know that with my B.A. in Force Theory I may seem overqualified for this position, but I've decided that I'm more interested in a life of adventure than a stable job with a reputable organization at this point in my career. I've dealt with my share of rough characters at my current job at Mos Eisley Spaceport Cantina and my neighborhood is pretty regularly terrorized by Tusken Raiders, so I don't think I'll have much trouble adjusting to the life of a bounty hunter. Please contact me as soon as is convenient for you, because I'm anxious to get started!

Sincerely,

Ken Skywalker

P.S. In case you're concerned about my academic background, I only attended the Tatooine Academy to get my parents off my back. Trust me when I say that I have learned that hokey religions and ancient weapons are no match for a good blaster at your side.

9/4

Jabba the Hutt, C.E.O., Hutt Enterprises, Inc.

Dear Mr. Hutt,

I recently learned of an opening with your crime syndicate here on Tatooine. I'm not sure what the job entails exactly, but I think I'm up for just about anything after working as the Assistant Manager of the Mos Eisley Cantina Spaceport. Since I was put in charge of marketing, we were named 2nd runner up for "Most Wretched Hive of Scum and Villainy" by the Imperial Travel Bureau. Although I've never killed anyone myself, I am often expected to clean up the charred corpses of bounty hunters and other scoundrels, and I'm becoming rather inured to the spectacle of mutilation and manslaughter.

I know I probably don't fit the typical profile of your applicants, but I think that if you give me a chance you won't be disappointed. All I'm asking for is a chance.

Eagerly awaiting your reply,

Ken S.

P.S. I don't need health insurance and I don't mind sleeping on the floor or whatever.

10/27

Dear Uncle Skip,

Do you still own that Chili's in the Dagobah system?

Your loving nephew,

Kenny

Harry Potter and the Inevitable Slide into Satanism

Before I became a parent, I was frequently amazed at the overprotectiveness of some people regarding their children. I don't mean parents who make their kids wear helmets while riding their bikes or solving a particularly difficult geometry problem; I'm talking about parents who won't let their kids read *Harry Potter* books or listen to music inspired by the devil. What, I thought to myself, are these parents afraid of exactly? Is there some kind of natural progression from J.K. Rowling fan to goat-worshiping cultist? Where does one turn in one's copy of Black Sabbath's *Born Again* for a black robe, ceremonial dagger and engram audit? Wait, that last one may be Scientology. I can't keep my evil religions straight any more.

Still, you get the point. I just couldn't see how kids went from dabbling in occult-inspired media to being full-fledged Satan worshipers. Or hell, even half-fledged. Half-fledged Satan worshipers are almost worse in a way, because they've got a chip on their shoulder and are just itching for a chance to earn their fledge.

Now that I'm a parent, I've realized the necessity of keeping certain books, movies and music away from my children. I don't like the idea of censorship, but no matter how much my kids beg they are not going to be allowed to listen to "Fergilicious" or read *Eragon*. I'm sorry, but I believe the children are our future.

Neither of my children (aged 6 and 8) have come home toting a Black Sabbath record yet, so I've dodged that bullet so far. But in anticipation of my eight-year-old bookworm eventually asking whether he may read *Harry Potter and the Nominative Phrase*, I decided to peruse one of these books to determine for myself whether there was any real danger.

I was shocked at what I discovered. In the back of the book was the following ad, reproduced here in its undoctored entirety.

☐ **YES!** *I'm a Harry Potter fan who is interested in becoming more involved in devil worship and the occult!*

Name:_____ Phone number:_____ Email:_____

Address:_____ City:_____ State:____ ZIP:_____

In addition to Harry Potter, I'm currently involved in the following demonic activities:
- ☐ Playing Dungeons and Dragons
- ☐ Listening to Marilyn Manson, Rob Zombie, Disturbed, or James Blunt
- ☐ Trying to speak with dead relatives at locations other than cemetery
- ☐ Teasing siblings until they cry

I am interested in:
- ☐ Summoning demon(s)
- ☐ Revenge on those who have transgressed against me
- ☐ Knowing the future
- ☐ Frightening teachers/parents

I am willing to get the following marks to demonstrate my devotion to Satan:
- ☐ Black nail polish
- ☐ Nose ring
- ☐ Tattoo of pentagram (NOT removable)
- ☐ 666 on forehead

What is your current religious affiliation:
- ☐ Born again Christian
- ☐ The other kind of Christian
- ☐ Catholic
- ☐ Jewish
- ☐ None/Science
- ☐ Other

Please contact me by:
- ☐ Phone
- ☐ Email
- ☐ Speaking through static on the TV
- ☐ Voices in my head

Are you interested in being possessed by a demon?*
- ☐ Yes
- ☐ No
- ☐ Maybe, on a trial basis

*Demonic possession generally entails vastly increased strength and resistance to physical harm, but may also cause projectile vomiting and loss of free will.

Please mail your completed form to:

Knights in Satan's Service
Attn: Harry Potter Department
666 Lucifer Way
Las Vegas, NV 66666-6666

TEAR ON DOTTED LINE

Can you believe that? I don't want my kids getting their hands on this kind of stuff!

Now where did I put those stamps?

Reality Bites

I don't watch reality TV because, after all, I watch television to escape reality, not to be subjected to more of it. The whole premise of reality TV seems misguided to me. How many people become drug addicts or alcholics because they just can't get enough reality?

Reality TV, of course, has about as much connection to actual reality as Court TV has to the reign of Louis VIX. I don't know about you, but a typical day for me is more likely to be dominated by Pointless Meetings and acid reflux than Immunity Challenges and secret alliances. The idea of people being sent to strange locales where they are made to engage in bizarre competitions isn't even original. It's called *sports*, and it was around long before Thomas Edison produced the first reality show, an intriguing little silent film called *Two Spaniards Dig a Medium-Sized Hole*. And no, I don't watch sports either. Still too much like real life to me. For me, the less like reality a show is, the better. If I only got two channels and one of them showed *Big Brother* and the other showed the *Teletubbies*, it would be time for Tubby Watch-Watch.

The idea behind reality TV seems to be that if you put enough cameras on enough ordinary people for a long enough period of time, something like a coherent narrative will emerge. This, the experiment unfortunately reveals, is bullsh*t. If you film a million monkeys flinging poo, they do not eventually by sheer chance construct Michelangelo's "David" out of poo. And even if they did, it would still be made of poo, a notoriously ephemeral medium. Most Americans can't even name a single 20th century artist who worked primarily in poo, a fact which cannot be attributed entirely to the failings of the school system.

If you want to watch ugly people do boring things, go to the mall. TV should be reserved for beautiful people kissing or shooting at each other. *The Amazing Race* has the right idea by making sure to include a couple of teams selected purely for their aesthetic qualities. If I were the producer of that show, it would be hella hard to follow because every team would get the caption "Friends/Models." But it wouldn't matter, because when everybody is pretty, everybody wins.

What I really don't get is *The Biggest Loser*. If you want to pull viewers in at the beginning of the season, don't start with fat, ugly people. Start with pretty people and gradually make them fat and ugly. You could give the contestants prizes for eating the most bacon-wrapped Twinkies or having the biggest self-inflicted oozing sore. The only thing viewers love more than watching pretty people is watching pretty people get punished for being pretty. *The Biggest Loser* is doubly irritating to me because I had the idea for that show a year before it debuted. The only difference was that in my version the fat people were going to be kidnapped off the street by teams who were competing to bag the biggest lardass they could find, and they'd get extra points for people wearing spandex or lycra. Then each team would train their fat person to run an obstacle course, which their contestant would have to run while the other teams shot at them with pellet guns.

Come to think of it, my version was quite a bit different.

Those of you who are my age may remember that reality TV started when producers were forced into airing more "unscripted" programs during a writer's strike during the late 80s. As I recall, sanitation workers in several major cities were striking around the same time, and the results of each strike were similar.

People generally cite *The Real World* as the beginning of the era of reality TV, but to me it all started with *Cops*. Now *there* was a reality show. No "characters," no "narratives," no back stories or conflict resolution. No sports either, unless you consider the 500 meter shirtless 'hood run a sport. Nothing but an endless parade of depravity and idiocy. I'm grateful for the lack of coherency on *Cops*. I don't want to know about these losers' tragic childhood or their inevitable incarceration, release, and recidivism. If you give me too much information, these stories become tragedies. I want to remember these people at their peak – as the guy who reported the theft of his pot stash to the cops, or the scrawny hippie dude who got the crap kicked out of him by his 400 pound wife. My all time favorite was the drunk guy who insisted he was a CIA agent. When the cop asked him if he could touch his nose with his fingertip, he dropped into a karate stance and said, "I can do *this!*"

Now if reality was more like *that*, I'd watch less TV.

Congratulations on Your New Testicles!

Congratulations!

You've just purchased a pair of novelty testicles for your truck, SUV or other vehicle.

With the purchase of this fine product you have joined the informal fraternity of novelty nutsack owners – the three million men (and possibly women, although we doubt it) whose vehicles already bear the unmistakable mark of supreme manliness. Yes, you've joined our proud brotherhood at the peak of its popularity, and whatever your reason for waiting so long, we're glad to have you aboard.

Frequently Asked Questions:

Q: I hear people making remarks about "compensating for some shortcoming." What does that mean?

A: These people are jealous. There is no documented evidence that novelty testicle owners suffer from any sort of physical inadequacy. In fact, during a recent door-to-door survey most novelty testicles owners reported having genitalia as large or larger than the national average.

Q: Some people roll their eyes and/or shake their heads when they see my testicles. Why?

These people don't "get it."

Q: The women I know tell me my testicles are stupid and lame.

A: They're lying. Women love novelty testicles. When they are in the bathroom together they talk about which guy has the biggest novelty testicles and try to figure how they can get that guy to have sex with them. A very small percentage of women really do think your testicles are lame. These women are college professors who think they're too good for you, or lesbians. Often they are both.

Q: I'm concerned that my novelty testicles may soon go "out of style."

A: There is no need to worry. Novelty testicles, like the mullet and decals of a little boy peeing on things, never get old.

Q: People with small children glare at me as they drive past. Am I doing something wrong?

No. You're not the problem here. This happens because little Brittany in the back seat has just asked, "Mommy, what are those?" Brittany has to learn some day, so it might as well be when she's in first grade.

Q: How do I keep people from stealing my novelty testicles?

A: We recommend coating your testicles with rancid bacon grease. This will also help prevent corrosion.

Q: I think my girlfriend is envious of my testicles. Do you have any products geared more toward women?

A: Absolutely! We are constantly adding new items to our Scrotowear collection. What better gift could there be than a genuine leather Scrotowear purse?

And for those really special occasions, break out a Scrotowear pendant or earrings!

Order them for her today. You know she wants it!

The Best Things in Life Are Free (Unless You Are Stupid)

They say the best things in life are free, but that sounds more like a lousy business model than a viable worldview to me. If they were really the best things, they would cost a lot more. Just try going to Best Buy and loading a 62" plasma into your car without paying for it. What kind of twisted worldview doesn't consider a top of the line Hi-Def Plasma TV as one of the best things in life? (I have to admit, though, that the police car ride was pretty fun and technically didn't cost me anything.)

Oh, I know, there's sunshine and oxygen and blah blah blah. But it's all supply and demand. You'd pay for oxygen if I was holding a plastic bag over your head, and if you don't believe me you can ask my little brother. (I just hope you have more money.) And if you've never paid for sunshine, you've obviously never lived in Grand Rapids, Michigan. Do you know how desperate for sunshine you have to be to pay someone $50 so you can lie in a coffin and be showered in cancer-causing radiation? There were days in January in Michigan when I would have paid someone to shove my face into a frying pan and call it a sunburn.

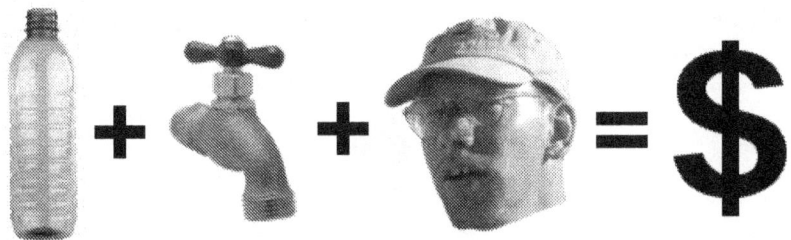

Some day I'm going to find a way to bottle sunshine. They already charge stupid people a dollar for a little bottle of water. And while people who can't figure out how to get water into a bottle apparently comprise a pretty big market, I'm willing to bet that the market for bottled sunshine is even bigger. The bottled water people are so stupid they don't even realize that Evian is "naive" spelled backwards. I'm going to call my bottled sunshine KramYsae or Ssabmud. Or maybe I should name it after the mystical source of the product, in the manner of Crystal Geyser or Ice Mountain. I'll call it, um, The Sun. Ooh, I know! I'll combine the two methods and call it "The Sun, Ssabmud."

You'll be happy to know that I did some intense research[*] on this subject, and I discovered that "All over the world, water is one of the most popular drinks." That's a bold statement. I'd like some additional supporting information. For example, do thirsty people drink more than non-thirsty people? Do people prefer to drink their water in liquid form, or inhale it as steam? How do people feel about drinking very dirty water, say, with cat urine and mercury in it?

I also learned that the difference between tap water and bottled water is that tap water comes out of a "tap," whereas bottled water is generally surrounded by a plastic container known as a "bottle." According to some reliable website that I don't feel like giving credit to, "Aquafina is municipal

---

[*] Google search

water from spots like Wichita, Kansas. Coke's Dasani is taken from the taps of Queens, New York, Jacksonville, Florida, and elsewhere. Everest bottled water originates from southern Texas, while Yosemite brand is drawn from the Los Angeles suburbs."

So if you're a health conscious Glendale resident breaking open a bottle of Yosemite, keep in mind that you've just paid someone a dollar to fill up a bottle with water from your kitchen sink. That's like paying a dollar for a little mirror so that you can go outside and enjoy the sunshine. Hey, that gives me an idea....

Don't Make Me Angry

The Incredible Hulk is different from most superheroes in that Bruce Banner[*] can't control when he turns into the Hulk. I guess Diana Prince couldn't fully control her transformation into Wonder-Woman either, but she was safe as long as she didn't turn around too fast. I think the idea was originally to make the Hulk sort of an anti-hero Jekyll-and-Hyde type guy. Remember how sad he looked, walking along the side of the road at the end of each show, hoping that the next leap would be the leap home? Wait, I think I'm confused. Anyway, it was really sad.

The problem with the Hulk concept is that despite his "curse," the Hulk's super-strength always came in pretty handy for old Doc Banner. You'd think that after the seventeenth time the Hulk saved his ass, he'd rethink his quest for a "cure" for his condition. I wish I could turn into the Hulk when somebody pissed me off. Like I'd be in a meeting, explaining what was going to happen when we rolled out an application that I'd been working on for six months, and somebody would say, "Whoa, we can't have it do that." And I'd say, "But that's exactly what you said you wanted it to do in the requirements meeting back in June." And then they'd say,

---

[*] He was actually named "David Banner" on the TV show, because the producers thought the alliteratively comic-booky "Bruce Banner" would detract from the serious tone of the show (In a way that a Lou Ferrigno covered in green powder breaking through Styrofoam bricks did not, presumably).

"Mmmmmm no, you must have misunderstood." And then I'd say, "Oh, did I misunderstand it when I wrote it up in a requirements document and sent it to you to review six months ago?" And they'd say, "Oh, I guess I didn't read that." And then I'd turn into the Hulk and rip out their spine through their abdomen. Or maybe just toss them through a paper-mache wall. Still, they'd get the idea.

Of course then everybody would know I was the Hulk, and they'd always be trying to get me to turn into the Hulk at parties and stuff. They'd be like, "Hey dude, did you hear that France has outlawed Arnold Schwarzenegger movies?" And I'd be like, "Oh no they didn't." And they'd be like, "Dude, it's totally true. That's just how evil they are." And I'd be like, "Pansy French bastards!" And they'd be like, "Yeah, doesn't that just make you SOOOOO angry?" And then I'd be like, "Hey, you're just trying to get me to turn into the Hulk again, like that time you told me Michael Moore was suing McDonald's for making him weigh 400 pounds." And they'd be like, "Oh come on, just do it. We brought a change of clothes for you."

Because if you were the Hulk, you'd go through a lot of clothes. I bet that's why he was so desperate for a cure. Remember, this was in the days before Costco, so he couldn't just buy 40 polyester-blend button-downs at a time. That's probably why he always had to hitch-hike too. You can't afford a car when you're shelling out $500 a week for new clothes. If I were him, I'd have just had a special Hulk-suit made out of whatever material was in his waistband. Talk about super-powers, he could have patented that waistband material. I mean, I have to unbutton my pants when I have too many yams at Thanksgiving, but his waistband could easily stretch to fit a man three times his size. And yet, those boot-cut slacks would split at the ankles. Curious.

I'd probably turn into the Hulk at really inappropriate times. Like the other day I dropped my tuna melt on the floor, so the cheese slid off and got all yucky. Man, I was so mad that I'd have turned into the Hulk for sure if I had it in me. Next thing I'd know, I'd wake up dazed and shirtless in my neighbor's orchard, craving a tuna melt but finding only rubble where my house had been. And that would make me so mad I'd turn into the Hulk again and smash the rubble into smaller rubble. This cycle would continue until I was too hungry and worn out to turn into the Hulk any more, and I'd have to drag my half-naked ass to Arby's for a Roast Beef and Cheddar. And the guys at Arby's would recognize me and be like, "Oh, we can't sell those any more because of the Michael Moore lawsuit." And I'd be like, "Guys, I'm not in the mood. Just give me the friggin' sandwich."

A Conversation Overheard in the Batcave

Robin: Hey, Batman, can I ask you a question?

Batman: Sure, Robin. What's up?

Robin: What's the thinking behind the whole bat motif?

Batman: Good question! Well, my young protégée, the idea is to strike fear into the hearts of criminals.

Robin: You mean because bats are scary. Kind of creepy and mysterious.

Batman: Exactly.

Robin: Makes sense. You wouldn't want to pick some kind of timid, innocuous creature for your avatar.

Batman: Yep, I made the right choice there.

Robin: And the color scheme?

Batman: Same deal. It's got to be dark to be scary.

Robin: Right, right. And I suppose it makes it harder to see you in the dark.

Batman: Indeed. Perfect camouflage.

Robin: Not like a brightly colored suit that anybody could see a mile off.

Batman: That's right. Don't want to get shot. This is a dangerous business.

Robin: Good thinking. And, ah, the tights? Are they just for show?

Batman: Of course not. They also keep me nice and warm in the cold Gotham winters.

Robin: Yeah, you'd have to be nuts to run around in your skivvies.

Batman: Can you imagine? Plus I'd look hella gay. Not exactly frightening.

Robin: Heh, heh. Yeah. And the mask? Is that for effect?

Batman: Mostly, but it also helps hide my identity. Gotta cover most of the face to keep from getting recognized.

Robin: Uh huh. And the cape? Any reason it has to be so big?

Batman: Oh man, this thing's a lifesaver. You have no idea how many times I've taken a header off a twenty story building with only my bat-cape to break my fall.

Robin: Can't get that kind of protection from a flimsy little yellow dishrag of a cape.

Batman: You've said a mouthful there, buddy.

Robin: I suppose it helps to have an indestructible vehicle.

Batman: Oh yeah, the Batmobile could take a direct hit from a rocket launcher. That thing's like a tank.

Robin: Ever thought of trading it in for something a little more nimble, like a motorcycle?

Batman: Good lord, no. Do you have any idea how vulnerable you are on a motorcycle? Any idiot with a slingshot could kill you on a motorcycle. You know, Robin, despite all the training I've given you, sometimes I think you're none too bright.

Superman Returns: The Unreleased Version

In Superman Returns, the Man of Steel reappears on Earth after a mysterious five year absence, during which he supposedly searched in vain for remnants of his home world, Krypton. We are led to believe that he was unable to find anything left of Krypton, but I have learned from highly placed sources at Warner Brothers that this aspect of the film was actually altered drastically during editing to make it shorter and more palatable to viewers. I have gotten my hands on the original script of the movie, which details Superman's trip to Krypton. An unedited excerpt appears below.

EXT. KRYPTON CITY. DAY.

Exotic buildings glitter in the ruddy glow of Krypton's red sun. A SPACE BUS marked "KRYPTON EXPRESS" lands at a SPACE BUS STOP. The doors open and several passengers wearing business suits exit. Among them is Superman, looking tired after a long journey. The bus takes off and the passengers disperse, leaving Superman standing alone at the bus stop with Steve, a shabbily dressed homeless Kryptonian.

Steve: Whoa, what's with the fancy duds, man?

Superman: Oh, it's sort of a costume. I'm Superman.

Steve: Nice. I like the black and red.

Superman: It's actually blue and red. It just looks black in this light.

Steve: What's "blue"?

Superman: Forget it. Can you tell me how to get to get to the El residence?

Steve: You mean Jor-El? Sure, I can tell you how to get there. He's my uncle.

Superman: Your uncle? Then you must be....

Steve: I'm Steve-El. Todd-El's kid.

Superman: Steve! It's me, your cousin Kal!

Steve: Kal? Holy crap, I haven't seen you since you were a baby! Where the heck have you been?

Superman: My dad sent me to Earth.

Steve: Earth? What the heck for?

Superman: I guess he thought Krypton was going to explode.

Steve: Explode! That's crazy!

Superman: He used to watch a lot of the *Krypton 700 Club* with Pat-Ro.

Steve: Wow. He always was a little nuts. Lately he's been wandering around in his bathrobe muttering something about "the horror."

Superman: So nothing here exploded?

Steve: Just the real estate market. If your dad had bought you a condo in Krypton City instead of a spaceship....

Superman: I know, I know. Don't remind me.

Steve: So what were you doing on Earth?

Superman: Oh, defeating supervillains, reversing the spin of the planet on its axis to turn back time, that sort of thing.

Steve: Seriously?

Superman: Oh yeah, I'm kind of a big deal on Earth.

Steve: How did you manage that?

Superman: Check this out: On earth Kryptonians have super-powers.

Steve: No shit?

Superman: No shit.

Steve: Like what?

Superman: Try flight, for starters. That's how I got here. Well, I had to take a bus the last few million miles because of the red sun....

Steve: The red sun interferes with your powers?

Superman: Well, I get my powers from a yellow sun.

Steve: Any yellow sun?

Superman: Pretty much.

Steve: And there have got to be...

Superman: Millions of them, yeah.

Steve: So if I had been born on basically any other planet than Krypton...?

Superman: You'd have super-powers, right. Ironic, isn't it? We were born on the one planet where our super-powers don't work.

Steve: Man, we got screwed.

Superman: That's not the half of it. You know those green crystals that are all over this place?

Steve: Death Rock, you mean?

Superman: Yeah, Death Rock. Believe it or not, Krypton is the only place in the galaxy that has it. The only way those chumps on earth have a chance against me is if they somehow get their hands on some of that stuff. They call it "kryptonite." Speaking of which, if Krypton didn't explode, where are those kryptonite meteors coming from?

Steve: Oh man, Krypton's scientists have been shooting Death Rock at Earth by the ton. Trying to get rid of it, you know. I don't think they knew you were there.

Superman: I should hope not.

Steve: So what other powers do you have?

Superman: See that building over there?

Steve: Don't tell me you could leap over that building.

Superman: I could pick that building up and throw it into the sun.

Steve: No freaking way.

Superman: I'm dead serious. Bullets bounce right off of me. I can see through anything except lead. Oh and I can make laser beams shoot from my eyes. But enough about me. What have you been up to?

Steve: Well, I got laid off from my job as a Phantom Zone guard, so lately I've been reassessing things. I've got an application in for a job removing Death Rock insulation from old buildings.

Superman: Wow. Sounds like you've really, ah, done well for yourself.

Steve: If I get the job, I could put in a good word for you.

Superman: Nah, that's ok. Actually, I've got a bus to catch.

Steve: But you just got here. I thought you were going to see Jor-El.

Superman: I just remembered something I need to take care of.

Steve: Really? What?

Superman: Well, I should probably check to see if they need me on Earth. September 10, 2001 was a long time ago. I have high hopes for the Bush administration to make some real progress toward world peace.

Steve: Hmmm...

Superman: Oh, I also meant to cash in my Enron stock before I left. I should get back before the market peaks.

Steve: Ok, well come back soon and let me know how it goes.

Superman: I'll sure try. You know how hard it is to get away from the yellow sun.

Brilliant! (James Blunt's Songwriting Journal)

"I wrote 'You're Beautiful' in two and a half minutes, after seeing an ex-girlfriend.'"

- James Blunt

Blunt said on VH1's *The V spot* that he wrote this song about seeing his ex-girlfriend with a new man in the London underground. He says that they shared a lifetime in the brief eye contact.

Excerpt From James Blunt's Songwriting Journal

Tuesday, January 18, 2005

2:37:30 PM

Train should be here in about 150 seconds. Maybe enough time to write a song???

2:37:36 PM

Possible song topics: Trains. Unemployment. Sodding London weather. Come on man, think!

2:37:42 PM

Isn't that Stacy?

2:37:48 PM

That IS Stacy! Who the f---- is she with???!!!

2:37:55 PM

Stacy be lookin FINE.

2:38:04 PM

Where was I? ... Trains, right. Maybe something about a little engine trying to get up a hill?

2:38:09 PM

Lucky bastard. What was it Mum said when Stacy broke up with me? "God's will." Well I hope the sodding angels are happy. Bollocks.

2:38:17 PM

Feeling very sad.

2:38:21 PM

VERY sad.

2:38:29 PM

Maybe write a song about how sad I feel. Free association time! Sad, sad, sad.... Think of something very sad. Clowns with frowny faces are sad. Sad clown. Clown crying. TEARS OF A CLOWN!

2:38:41 PM

F---.

2:38:50 PM

She looked at me! HI Stacy!!!! GOD I'M SO HAPPY.

2:38:58 PM

Don't think she recognized me. SO SAD. This is the saddest anybody has ever been.

2:39:06 PM

Sadder than Bruce Banner walking away at the end of The Incredible Hulk.

2:39:14 PM

Damn, now I have that song in my head. Bah-bada-Bah. Bah-bada-Bah BAH.

2:39:22 PM

LOL. Should write lyrics about Stacy and that sodding bastard set to Incredible Hulk theme. F---, that's brilliant!

2:39:31 PM

Train's coming! Write something. ANYTHING!

My life is brilliant.
My love is pure.
I saw an angel
of that I'm sure
She smiled at me on the subway.
She was with another man.
But I won't lose any sleep on that
Cause I got a plan
You're beautiful; you're beautiful:
You're beautiful; it's true
I saw your face in a crowded place
And I don't know what to do
Cause I will never be with you
Yeah, she caught my eye
As I walked on by
She could see from my face that I was
Flying high
And I don't think that I'll see her again
But we shared a moment that will last till the end
You're beautiful; you're beautiful:
You're beautiful; it's true
I saw your face in a crowded place
And I don't know what to do
Cause I will never be with you
la la la la
la la la la
la la la la la
You're beautiful; you're beautiful
You're beautiful; it's true
There must be an angel with a smile on her face
When she thought up that I should be with you
But it is time to face the truth
I will never be with you

2:40:00 PM

Train's here!

Bringing Snarky Back

Although I engaged in my share of mischief when I was a kid, one thing I don't remember having to be told was to wear clothes that fit me. I was never tempted to wear pants that were 6 sizes too big so that they had to be held up with an elaborate system of safety pins and duct tape. Maybe I was brainwashed by "the man," but my teenage rebellion never reached the level where I felt like everybody needed to see my Rocky and Bullwinkle boxers. For that matter, I always put my arms through both shirt sleeves and wore my shoes on the correct feet. I know, I'm a sheep.

So let me just come out and say it: I don't understand kids these days. I try to stay up on what's "hip" and "cool." I make a real effort to drive like an idiot while listening to loud music with my windows rolled down so that I'll stay young at heart and/or die in an exciting explosion. I've always believed that it's better to burn out than to fade away, and my health plan confirms this fact. But I just don't understand this generation.

I mean, what's with music these days? I'll grant you that my generation will have to answer for Tone Loc and Debbie (sorry, Deborah!) Gibson. But have you listened to some of the crap on the radio today? And I'm not just talking about Fifty Cent's admonitions to lick his "lollipop," or Fergie from the Black Eyed Peas singing about her "lovely lady lumps." (Am I the only one who finds the use of the word "lump" in a pop song about the female anatomy profoundly disturbing? I'm militantly heterosexual, and even the lollipop sounds more appetizing to me. *Shudder...*).

Sickeningly graphic lyrics aside, what really bothers me about these songs is the horrifically bad writing. For example, these are the lyrics to an actual pop song by something called "Cascada":

> Your arms are my castle
> Your heart is my sky
> They wipe away tears that I cry

I'm not sure what I should expect from a group whose name sounds more like a brand of bottled water than a pop act, but do I actually need to make the point that Mad Libs are not an adequate inspiration for song lyrics? I imagine the group working feverishly on earlier versions of the song, something like:

> Your spleen is my pillow
> Your scalp is my hat
> They scare the hell out of my cat.

Don't get me wrong, I'm ok with the arms = castle metaphor. It's a little harder to figure out how heart = sky, but I could let that go as a standard bad pop song lyric. But when in the history of humankind has anyone ever wiped their tears away with ANY of those things? If you made me list every possible thing that I might conceivably wipe my face with, the only one of these items that would be in the top 500 is "arms." The other three would fall below just about anything that isn't sharp or poisonous.

And don't get me started on Justin Timberlake's "Sexy Back." No, the song is not about Justin's fuzz-covered back. Rather, it's what he's going to bring, to wit:

> I'm bringing sexy back
> Them other boys don't know how to act
> I think you're special what's behind your back
> So turn around and I'll pick up the slack.

That's right, he had to rhyme "back" with "back" because he couldn't think of another word that fit. I know, how about *hack*?

What really bothers me about "Sexy Back," however, is that while it sounds like it probably had about 28 producers, not one of them remembered to bring the melody. The song is like a ragtag collection of sound samples that showed up at the recording studio and waited as long as they could for the melody to show up, and then finally decided to go on without it. The result is about as interesting as The Doors without Jim Morrison. Or talent. The first time I heard this song I spent a minute and a half wondering when it was going to start, and then, when I realized it wasn't, spent another minute and a half praying desperately for it to end.

In any case, does sexy really need to be brought back? Where has it been, and what Justin was doing with it while he was out?

To be honest, I hadn't noticed sexy had even gone missing, but then I'm pretty old.

5

Politics and Current Events

In which the reader is instructed not only what to think, but how to think it.

One problem with being as smart as I am is that people are always asking for my opinions on things. I get asked all the big questions, like "Are you even listening to me?", "Where are you going with this?" and "Are you about finished?"

When I first started blogging, I wrote a lot about politics, because what the world desperately needed at the dawn of the 21st century was yet another blowhard telling people what to think. It took a while, but eventually I was able to align my entire readership to my point of view. I did this by gradually alienating readers who disagreed with me. Once I had accomplished this goal, my readers and I shared a six-pack and went our separate ways (don't worry, I took a cab).

I no longer write political commentary *per se*. I don't attack conservatives for being conservatives or liberals for being liberals. I generally don't even attack stupid people for being stupid. Stupid people are just people, like you and me. Except they vote for Al Sharpton.

These days if I touch on politics, it's only because the political arena is so rich with absurdity that it's just about impossible not to occasionally make fun of it. To the extent that I write political commentary now, it's only to attack what I see as willful ignorance and obtuseness. I don't make fun of George W. Bush, because I think he's a well-meaning guy who's a little out of his depth. And by "a little out of his depth," I mean that when I see him at a press conference these days it's like I'm watching one of those stories on CNN where a four year old falls into a well and the whole town works for like three days to get him a sandwich. And then he chokes on it. And I'm saying this as someone who voted for the guy. Twice. (Although to be fair, the second time I thought I was voting for Pat Buchanan.)

So this chapter isn't so much about my political opinions as it is a reaction to the deliberate stupidification of our political process. The point of this chapter isn't to make you into a bunch of clones of me. It's to make you into my unquestioning minions, who choose to believe what I believe out of their own free will.

I'm a multiplier, not a divider.

Fed Chair Speaks Out Against Smiley Inflation

WASHINGTON, November 27 — Ben S. Bernanke, chairman of the Federal Reserve, warned Monday that recent inflation trends were "unwelcome developments," indicating that he was particularly worried about a relatively recent phenomenon known as "smiley inflation."

In his toughest comments yet about the risks of smiley inflation, Mr. Bernanke said Internet users were utilizing smileys and chat abbreviations such as "LOL" and "ROTFL" at unprecedented rates. He indicated that while rising consumer prices were of moderate concern, what really worried him was the "irrational exuberance" regarding smileys characterizing the current market landscape.

Fed chair Ben Bernanke answers questions on the overuse of smileys.

"Five years ago, the basic unit of currency exchanged for a moderately amusing remark was a regular smiley (:)), grin smiley (:D) or a simple 'heh.' These units were rapidly devalued and were soon replaced by the laughing smiley (:))) or LOL. Now there is an increasing prospect of serious LOL devaluation, which has a lot of people concerned."

Bernanke stopped short of saying the Fed would take decisive action to combat smiley inflation. As of Monday, the Federal Smiley Use rate remained unchanged at 36.3%, meaning that roughly a third of absurd announcements by government officials would continue to be followed by a single smiley, wink smiley (;)) or eye-rolling smiley (8-|). Use of devil smileys (>:)) and tongue-sticking-out smileys (:p) also remained unchanged at 12.5%, despite pressure from the Bush administration to raise this rate.

Bernanke would not comment on reports that the Treasury is considering the release of several additional high-end smileys. "For now," Bernanke said, "We believe that ROTFL and LMAO remain sufficient for most humorous transactions." He added that while the regular smiley has been devalued almost to the level of the dot (.), there remain some smileys, such as the clown (:o)) and crazy smiley (8-}), that are inexplicably underused. "We think it's sort of a Sacagawea dollar situation," Bernanke said. "Is it a dollar? Is it a quarter? Nobody really knows what to make of some of these smileys, and that lack of certainty pushes up the use of LOL and ROTFL." The real worry, however, is that overuse of these abbreviations will cause users to resort to increased use of ROTFLOL and ROTFLMAO. If ROTFLMAO becomes devalued, many analysts believe the Treasury will be forced to release new smileys or abbreviations.

A recent Congressional Smiley Committee report had suggested the gradual introduction of several new smileys, including:

:(~)   Laughing so hard you can see that thingy hanging down in the back of my throat.

:^&))   Laughing so hard that milk is shooting out of my nose.

:-[X=| Laughing so hard that I wet myself.

:)) [+]   Laughing so hard that paramedics had to be called.

:)) $$$ Laughing so hard that I expect to be paid for it.

The committee declined to endorse the so-called "nuclear option," the release of FTIEH (Funniest Thing I Ever Heard). Committee members cited concerns that it left no room for future abbreviations of even greater value.

"The work of the Smiley Committee is appreciated, but I believe it is premature to be talking about the need for more high-value smileys," Bernanke said. He is known for holding the controversial opinion that the level of humor on the Internet has actually been decreasing over recent years, despite the proliferation of smileys. His remarks on this subject have fueled concerns regarding the possibility of a "humor bubble." Smiley inflation occurs when there are "too many smileys chasing too few really funny jokes," Bernanke stated. "There are a lot of markets where users are throwing out LOLs in response to 'Garfield'-level humor. I don't believe that's sustainable over the long term."

Bernanke was asked to comment on an IM conversation between two office workers that made news over the weekend. The chat log, which was leaked to the press by an anonymous employee of AOL Time Warner, has created a firestorm of controversy regarding the company's alleged encouragement of the blatant overuse of smileys. The chat log reads, in part:

SidneyJennings2003: what r u doing this wkend?

KarenN1970: wacthing gilmor grlz. U?

SidneyJennings2003: LOL! me 2

KarenN1970: LOL ur 2 funny. is austin coming over???

SidneyJennings2003: we broke up

KarenN1970: OMG no way!!! :(:(:(

SidneyJennings2003: hes a big jerk i borke up with him!!!

KarenN1970: ROTFLMAO!!! ur 2 funny!! :D

"I don't see how anyone can look at an exchange like that and conclude that it represents a reasonable usage of smileys or abbreviations," Bernanke said.

Tim Kellerman, Vice President of AOL Time Warner for :D, dismissed the controversy. "Everyone knows that young female office workers use a ridiculous number of smileys," Kellerman said. "The market discounts it." He argued the use of smileys among users of all demographics remains well within historical norms. He added, "We're feeling very good about the level of use of smileys overall :) ."

The market's reaction to Bernanke's statement was mixed, with most Fed watchers expressing ":|" or "(:|".

World's Worst Dictator

Like most people, I rely on *Parade* magazine to provide me with some geopolitical perspective, not to mention recipes for hearty halftime meals for my Super Bowl party. (Actually, I rely on my wife for both of those things, but she in turn relies on *Parade*. And just because I couldn't tell you who played in the Super Bowl to save my life doesn't mean I don't need a hearty halftime meal, so get off my back.)

So it turns out that the world's worst dictator is some dude named Omar al-Bashir. He runs a little country club and spa called Sudan. You may have heard something about it in between Anna Nicole Smith's breasts. Er, in between stories about Anna Nicole Smith. And her breasts. Her non-biodegradable breasts.

Interlude: 3007 A.D: Archaeologists are excavating Anna Nicole Smith's grave.

Archaeologist 1: Hey, I found something.

Archaeologist 2: What is it?

Archaeologist 1: Guess.

So this guy, this "Worst Dictator in the World," has killed at least 180,000 civilians in Darfur and driven 2 million people from their homes. My question is, what exactly are they looking for in a dictator? I mean, this guy's no Hitler, but who is? Except Stalin, I mean. Stalin was pretty much Hitler.

But those two guys really skew the curve for the rest of the dictators. I think that you'd have to say, all things considered, that this Omar al-Bashir character is a pretty good dictator. I can see how he'd lose some points for limiting himself to sub-Saharan Africa, but you play the cards you're dealt. Give him some time.

You know who's a lousy dictator? Al Gore. First of all, he's kind of whiny and non-threatening. Second, he doesn't really run anything. Third, he keeps trying to "build consensus" and win people over with "appeals to reason." Let me tell you, *Earth in the Balance* is no *Mein Kampf*. And Davis

Guggenheim is no Leni Riefenstahl. And, uh, Tipper is no Eva Braun. That's what I've heard, anyway. You know how guys talk.

Al Gore missed a key opportunity when he claimed to have invented the Internet. He should have claimed to have invented the Spanish Inquisition. Or something even worse, like syphilis. Tell me you'd risk crossing the guy who's in charge of syphilis.

"Dude, you look terrible! What happened to you?"

"Oh, man. I voted against Kyoto and Al Gore gave me syphilis."

And now he's gone and gotten himself nominated for a Nobel Peace Prize. I know, I know, Yasser Arafat got the Nobel Peace Prize and he was a murderous terrorist bastard. But still, there's a cachet of pacifism that goes with getting the Nobel Peace Prize. It's unfair, especially since Al Gore doesn't deserve all the credit for preventing the Great Global Warming War. I mean, shouldn't some of the credit go to the millions of individuals on both sides who aren't fighting? There's no way that Al Gore could have single-handedly prevented the war if all those people refused to work within the political process to find a solution.

Ah, but history doesn't want to hear about the faceless men and women who are ignorant of the conflict they could be participating in. Besides, the faceless are notoriously poor combatants. History remembers the Great Men with Faces, like Al Gore and what's his face in the Sudan.

Oops, gotta go. Anna Nicole's boobs are on!

Can't We All Just Get Along?

It seems to me that there is a lot of unnecessary strife in this world of ours. Wouldn't it be great if we could eliminate the petty disagreements among us and live like the brothers and sisters we are in the great family that is humanity? This post is my humble attempt to encourage all of us, whatever our ethnicity, political persuasion, gender, or attitude toward pork products, to put aside our petty differences and focus on what unites us as a species. This is just one simple American's take on things, but I think if everybody would make an effort to follow these simple guidelines, we could make the world a better place.

1. **Speak English.** Imagine how many misunderstandings we could prevent if everybody would just speak English. Pretty much everybody important speaks English these days, so there's no point in sticking with whatever doomed language your parents are trying to foist on you. What language did Shakespeare write in? English. What language are the ten most popular movies of all time in? English. What language is the Bible written in? English. The other day I saw something on TV where two kids in Holland were speaking Hollandaise to each other. Now I know for a FACT they teach English in schools in Holland. So these kids were obviously just trying to be provocative. Speaking a foreign language when everybody knows you speak English just raises suspicion. You saw what we did to Iraq; don't be stupid.

2. **Use dollars.** Everything important is denominated in dollars these days, and frankly your hexagonal coins with the hole in the middle and your paper money with Queen Amidala on one side and a purple chicken on the other are just plain embarrassing. This is especially the case for those of you from countries that peg your currency to the dollar anyway. Your economy is too unstable to support your own currency but we're supposed to be impressed by the portrait of Jose What's-his-name on your peso? Do you know how big the U.S. national debt is? Five *trillion* dollars. So do you want a piece of that action or are you really going to stick with the purple chicken? Yeah, that's what I thought.

3. **Drive on the right side of the road.** You know why it's called the "right" side of the road? Because it's the right side to drive on. That's pretty straightforward. I don't mean to be overly harsh, but we invented cars, so we get to decide. If you invent something we'll let you decide how it works.

4. **Be respectful of normal people's lifestyles.** If you're gay, or Hindu, or vegetarian, or whatever, that's great. But keep it to yourself, would you?

5. **Stop using the metric system.** Our system is WAY easier, trust me. There are 12 inches in a foot, three feet in a yard, and a hundred yards in a football field. Simple, right?

6. **Stop making us ask permission to fly over your country.** We have important shit to do on the other side. You wouldn't understand.

7. **Stop making Mexican food that tastes like crap.** I am really tired of food in foreign countries not tasting like it's supposed to. You people in South America are particularly bad. You seem to think you can improve on Chevy's. Well, you can't. First of all, you don't use enough cheese. Good rule of thumb: You can never have too much cheese. Also, nobody likes corn tortillas. Chevy's would probably fly somebody down to help you out if you're having trouble.

8. **Stop making your own movies.** You don't have enough money to make them any good. And nobody wants to read a movie (see #1). We don't mind making the movies for you. Also, music and TV. And books, magazines, and software. Consider it our gift to you.

9. **Show some appreciation.** We don't mind defending the whole free world from the Nazis, Communists and Islamofascists. But it would be a nice gesture if you would say thank you once in a while. Maybe have a parade for us. Oh, and you could pick up a check occasionally.

10. **Use the term "American" correctly.** I know that this is kind of confusing, so I thought I would get it out in the open for once. Here's the deal: People from the United States of America are called Americans. I don't make the rules, but that's the way it is. There's really nothing else you could call us. United Statians? No, we're Americans. Which means that nobody else can be Americans. If you live in North America and you're not American, then you're Canadian. And if you live in South America, then you're Hispanic or, more formally, Mexican. Pretty easy when someone explains it, right?

Peace and goodwill toward all of you, especially those living in backward countries where you don't have a bicameral legislature or Wal-Mart.

2020 Vision

Campaign season gets longer and longer with every election, and using simple high school calculus and some PhD-level guesswork, I have extrapolated from current trends to determine that by the year 2020 campaign season will be roughly thirteen years long. In other words, to have a chance of winning the presidency in 2020, a candidate will have to have begun campaigning no later than 3 o'clock this afternoon.

It is with this in mind, love of my country in my heart, and a song in my pancreas, that I declare my candidacy for presidency of the United States. My slogan is *Diesel in 2020: No Special Rights for Cyborgs.*

My campaign is going to be built on a pledge of straight talk. Not that there's anything wrong with any other kind of talk; I just don't happen to swing that way. To demonstrate my straight-talkingness, here is where I stand on the "big issues:"

A Woman's Right to Choose

I strongly support a woman's right to choose. It should go without saying that I also support a man's right to choose. To my way of thinking, they should take turns. For example, first the man might choose a nice restaurant for them to go to. Then the woman could choose a top to go with her beige capri pants without asking the man whether he likes the blue one or the green one better. Then the man might choose to have cheesecake for dessert, and the woman might choose to get her own cheesecake rather than eat all of the man's. Only in this way can we build a truly just society.

Term Limits

I am strongly in favor of term limits. The term "diva," for example, has gotten way out of hand. Mariah Carey is a diva now? I don't think so. That's one term that needs some serious limits. And what about "shock jock"? Can we retire that one yet?

Flag Burning

A lot of people say flag burning isn't a serious issue, because hardly any actual flag burning takes place. These people are missing the point. The point is that without a law forbidding flag burning, anyone could hypothetically burn a flag whenever he or she sees fit. And that's what I have a problem with: the hypothetical flag burning. I believe that we should not only outlaw burning flags; we should also outlaw the *hypothetical* burning of flags. Let's say, for example, that you were to burn a flag in your backyard. Under a typical anti-flag burning law, you would go to jail. But under my enhanced anti-flag burning law, you and I would *both* go to jail: You for burning the flag, and me for suggesting a hypothetical situation in which you burned the flag. And there we would sit, in our respective jail cells – mine real, yours hypothetical – reflecting on our respective real and imaginary crimes.

The War on Terror

I am strongly in favor of the War on Terror. In fact, I think the War on Terror should be drastically expanded to include all other unpleasant states of mind, such as Boredom and "the Heebie Jeebies." I don't think we should stop fighting until we are all happy all of the time. But we must stop before we hit Complacency, because the war will be on that too.

Campaign Finance Reform

The cost of national elections is obscene. It is estimated that the 2020 presidential campaign will cost more than the GDP of Canada. This is money that is going to lobbyists and marketing firms, when we could better use it to actually buy Canada. Sure, we don't need it now, but you never know what might happen down the road. What if Canada decides to slap an embargo on comedians? Not only will we miss out on any future Jim Carreys and Mike Myerses, but we will be unable to ship Jim Carrey and Mike Myers back to Canada when they turn into Robin Williams in a few years. Then you'll be wishing we bought Canada, won't you?

Iraq

I think we should "stay the course" in Iraq, because when you're bogged down in the desert, the best solution is generally a nautical metaphor. Some say that we're stuck between the devil and the deep blue sea, and that we should pull up anchor and rid ourselves of this albatross, but I say these people should stop rocking the boat and get on board with the program. We're still learning the ropes in Iraq, and I say that we need to batten down the hatches and throw those insurgents overboard. Fail in Iraq? Not on my watch. We're going to win, come hell or high water.

I hope I have convinced you that I have the kind of decisiveness and vision that is needed in 2020. Ooh, I like that. "Vision in 2020." Maybe that's my slogan. Oh well, there's plenty of time to work that out. The important thing is that Americans put aside their differences and agree to send me money for my campaign. That's the kind of unity I could celebrate.

I'd love to stick around and answer questions, but I'm three sheets to the wind already.

Talk Like a Man

Note: This seemed like a big deal at the time.

So everybody is talking about this Don Imus guy, and what a shame it is that after being on the radio for 40 years, he accidentally slipped up and said something offensive and got fired for it. The remarkable thing to me is that he evidently avoided saying anything offensive for nearly 40 years. Can you imagine talking for three hours a day for 40 years and never saying anything offensive? You should get some kind of medal for that. Even Moses lost his temper after 40 years of shtick on the wilderness circuit.

On the other hand, imagine being one of Imus' faithful listeners, anxiously awaiting the latest G-rated words of wisdom from their beatific role-model, only to be subjected to hate-filled epithets such as "nappy-headed hos." Can you imagine the shock these listeners must have felt? I mean, it's bad enough to refer to a group of respectable young women as "hos." Having lived in a deep well on an Amish beet farm for the past 18 years, I have never heard such language. I have never, for example, heard a man refer to his girlfriend or wife as a ho. I've never heard a woman refer to her friends as hos. I've never heard a white woman refer to a black woman as a ho, nor a black woman refer to a white woman as a ho. I have never heard two women of mixed race jokingly calling each other hos, nor a pair of conjoined twins referring to their adopted lesbian parents as hos. And I most certainly never heard six Chinese women calling seventy-eight Pakistani midgets and their albino monkey hos. And if I *had* ever heard the word "ho" used in any of these contexts, I would have been outraged *each and every time*, because if there's one thing I can't stand, it's intolerance.

Anyway, a lot of people seem to be ready to pull the plug on talk radio and replace it with something less offensive, like rap music. But being the high-minded and judicious person I am, I decided to find out what the fuss was all about. So I listened to some "talk radio" for a few hours one day. The show I found most interesting talked about the "homosexual agenda." Have you heard about this? It was a real eye-opener for me. I mean, I know that they tend to be detail-oriented, but who knew they had an actual *agenda*? That's just cool. I wish straight people had an agenda. As far as I know, the only thing we've agreed on is to split up boy/girl. If there's any kind of schedule for where or when we're supposed to do this, nobody's shown it to me. Let me tell you, if they had, it would have spared me some awkward moments in college.

The radio show didn't go into specifics, but several items on the gay agenda are evidently related to corrupting the youth and destroying America. For my gay readers: I hope you don't mind me saying this, but it seems like you're going a bit beyond your charter with stuff like this. After all, it's every person's right to want to corrupt the youth and destroy America, but I just don't see what any of that has to do with being gay. I pictured the gay agenda being something like this:

4:30	Hair appointment
5:10	Buy new shoes
6:00	Drinks with Steve!

I know you're probably not supposed to do this, but if you're gay and you're reading this, I'd really appreciate it if you could send me a copy of the agenda. Don't worry, I'm not going to publish it or anything. I'm just hoping to get some ideas for the straight agenda. Also, I'm wondering what the timetable is for abolishing the nuclear family and gayifying all of us breeders. Because if I'm going to be turned gay like next week, I really need to start doing some sit-ups or something.

Maybe I should start a radio show. I could raise concerns about all kinds of groups that I find a little suspicious. Like, what are those Shriners up to exactly? I mean, we all love kids, but doesn't it seem like they love kids a little *too* much? And the weird little cars. Sure, they claim that they're just for parades, but how long before you're stuck behind one of those damn things on I-5? You see where I'm going with this. What's the Shriner *agenda*?

The key to the show's success would be to never actually talk to any Shriners. Or, if I did talk to one, it would only be to demonstrate how the Shriner agenda is Wrong for America.

Diesel: Isn't it true, sir, that the Shriners want to destroy all that is good and decent about America?

Shriner Dude: Actually, we're a charitable organization that funds —

Diesel: Silence! What about the allegations that your group is an offshoot of the secretive order of the Knights Templar?

Shriner Dude: Well, originally the purpose of the Shriners was to protect the —

Diesel: I've heard enough of your lies! I'm only going to ask you this once: WHERE ARE YOU HIDING THE HOLY GRAIL?

Shriner: The Holy... I'm sorry, but I didn't expect this sort of Spanish Inquisition.

Michael Palin: NO ONE EXPECTS THE SPANISH INQUISITION!

I have some more stuff worked out, but I'd better not go into details before I've confirmed the availability of Graham Chapman. So for now, I can only offer a very rudimentary outline of the show. I'm thinking something like:

    4:30 News update
    5:10 Weather and traffic
    6:00 Drinks with Steve!

Harvard to Settle Question of God's Existence

Officials at Harvard University today announced a bold experiment designed to settle once and for all the question of God's existence.

Recently Harvard has come under fire for rejecting a recommendation that all undergraduates be required to take a class in religion. Now the university has released a statement that attempts to clear up the confusion regarding the policy.

"Our motivation is quite simply to test scientifically the hypothesis of God's existence," says Dr. Harold Emmets, the Harvard Dean of Reason and Objectivity. "The plan is to remove all vestiges of religion from Harvard and see if God goes medieval on our asses in retribution. If the campus is subjected to a series of disastrous plagues, we'll know that there is a God after all. Once it is agreed by the executive committee that the hypothesis has been confirmed, we will repent of the evil that is in our hearts and institute mandatory religious indoctrination for all students.

"If, however, Harvard continues to remain plague-free, we will require all students to take a class called '"Why Harvard is More Powerful than God."' Either way, Emmet notes, once the experiment is complete all students will be required to take a class dealing with religion.

In response, fundamentalist leader Pat Robertson immediately called for all "true Christians" to begin praying for the immediate and gruesome destruction of Harvard. "Break out your weenies," Robertson told a cheering crowd of several hundred enthusiastic listeners who had camped out just off-campus, "Because there's gonna be a fire."

Robertson said that God told him the exact time and date of Harvard's destruction, as well as the method the Almighty would use. "I think He said He was going to send a ball of fire from the pits of Gehenna. But He might have said 'boys choir from the city of Vienna.' Unfortunately, my hearing hasn't been so great since God visited His retribution upon me for listening to Pat Boone on my iPod a few weeks ago."

Despite the lack of certainty regarding the exact manner of grotesque punishment God would use, the crowd was on the verge of ecstasy anticipating the imminent destruction of the belligerently secular university.

One excited spectator was Josh Beeman, an Atlanta businessman and real estate mogul. "When the fire goes out and the German kids leave, I'm going to rush in and plant this on Harvard yard," Beeman said, holding a small flagpole bearing a hand-made flag with felt pictures of Jesus, the cross, and the Bible glued to it. "Once the land has been reclaimed for God," we're going to open a theme park called Conversion Land. We're going to have a swimming pool that can handle five hundred baptisms at a time and an authentic working replica of Heaven."

Harvard officials seemed frightened and confused regarding the gathering. "What do they want?" asked a bewildered physics professor. "Should we give them food?"

Visiting anthropology professor Jamaresh Hwarindi theorized that perhaps the protesters were "realizing the manifestation of the meta-societal dialectical process expressed in the collective recognition of the existential threat of the other."

In an uncanny parallel to HwarindI's statement, Robertson suggested the Harvard faculty were "possessed by a legion of demons from the blackest pit of hell."

Hwarindi admitted that he was puzzled by the protesters' behavior. "I just can't figure out what's motivating them," he said. "All of their material needs seem to be met, and yet they are clearly angered by something. Man, it's times like this that I wish I had taken a class in that, whatayacallit, *re-li-jun*."

As of midnight, the two sides had made no progress in the stalemate. Their only point of agreement was that neither side should make any attempt to directly engage the other in meaningful dialogue. Protesters burned copies of Harvard's statement without even reading it. "You don't need to lift the manhole cover to know the sewer stinks," said one.

In stark contrast, a statement by the protesters was greeted by the Harvard faculty with great enthusiasm. First the statement was ridiculed for its poor grammar and usage, then deconstructed in the light of a feminist Marxian framework, and finally recycled into rolling paper.

One department chair, who asked to remain anonymous, was heard to exclaim, "Whoa, that's good dogma."

Bush Fiddles While Moon Deteriorates

"Today, the Moon is 239,000 miles away from Earth and is moving further away. If left unabated the Moon would continue in its retreat until it would take about 47 days to orbit the Earth.... The Sun's mutation into a red giant is likely to ensure the Moon ends its days the way it began; as a ring of Earth-girdling debris. The density and temperature both increase rapidly near the surface of the future giant Sun. As the Earth and Moon near this blistering hot region, the drag caused by the Sun's extended atmosphere will cause the Moon's orbit to decay. The Moon will swing ever closer to Earth until the gravity holding it the Moon

together is weaker than the tidal forces acting to pull it apart. The Moon will be torn to pieces."

- From an article appearing on Space.com on January 22, 2007

In a ritual that is becoming all too familiar, scientists have once again announced troubling news from outer space. Despite repeated assurances from the Bush administration regarding prospects for long term lunar stability, it appears that the moon continues to disintegrate.

"At this point there seems to be little we can do," said Hans VerHoeven, director of the non-profit Council on Lunar-American Relations. After millennia of being pounded by meteors, VerHoeven noted, the moon finally appears near total collapse. "Yet the Bush administration insists that we must 'stay the course' with regard to the moon," VerHoeven added. "It's insane."

Terran Imperialism

Critics on both sides of the aisle have roundly criticized the Bush plan to require the Moon to continue to orbit the Earth at its present distance and velocity. "Release Earth's grip on the moon NOW!" read signs at a recent protest march which inexplicably occurred at a Taco Bell outside Redding, California. Denouncing "Terran imperialism" has become a favorite rallying cry of those who sympathize with the suffering of the uninhabited sphere.

Today the surface of the moon is lifeless and barren.

"First we send probes there looking for water," said Susan Jarvis, an unemployed Redding resident who attended the rally with her three unemployed children. "Well, guess what? There's no water. It was all lies. At least no planets disintegrated when Clinton lied about the Alpha Centaurians telling him to shag Gennifer Flowers."

An American flag now waves unnaturally over the previously

pristine surface of the Moon, a harsh reminder of Earth's past meddling in the region's politics. The nonexistent locals, who might once have welcomed Earth's superior technology in their fight against the constant barrage of space debris, are now strangely silent. The schools are empty, lacking even buildings to signify their presence. The playgrounds are indistinguishable from the nearby cornfields, in which no corn grows. And every square foot of the benighted satellite bears the scars of billions of years of neglect and an atmosphere even thinner than Earth's tired promises to "send another expedition" some day.

Not everyone blames Earth for the Moon's problems, however. Ted Barnett, a student at Chico State University, was angered by the protesters. "Everybody talks about how much light we get from the Moon," he said. "Nobody bothers to mention how light the Moon gets from *us*. Now get out of my way so I can get a f---ing gordita, for f---'s sake."

If You Are Indifferent to Something, Set It Free

The Bush administration has belatedly announced a plan to allow the Moon to slip 1.6 inches further away from the Earth per year, letting Earth's rotation slow gradually over the next 5 billion years. Critics argue that this is "too little, too late," and point out that the plan has to be renewed by Congress every four years. Democrats are worried that if they lose control over the House of Representatives at any time over the next five billion years, conservative Republicans will attempt to reassert Terran supremacy over the Moon.

"We've learned that you can't trust these lunocons," said Jarvis. "We've wasted enough of our gravity trying to hold onto a Moon that doesn't want our help. It's the same old story."

Is The Tide Turning?

Jarvis' own story goes deeper, however. It turns out that her son was Joseph "Woogie" Jarvis, a surfer who disappeared in a massive wave off Maui. She bristles at the idea that she is protesting out of anger at her son's Moon-related death. "My son's death was tragic," she says, "But the bigger issue here is, why is the Moon in our gravitational sphere in the first place?"

Like an increasing number of disillusioned citizens, Jarvis drives a car bearing a bumper sticker that reads "Support the Surfers – Release the Moon." She dismisses the contention that the moon might disintegrate even more rapidly if it is released from the Earth's gravity.

"That's a lie promoted by the Moon-mongers at Haliburton," Jarvis argues. Haliburton, the profiteering firm formerly run by Dick Cheney, has recently come under fire for rumors that it is building a gigantic evil base on the dark side of the moon, where it will be free from international scrutiny, heavy corporate taxes and five sixths of its current weight.

The Dark Side of Moon Policy

"Of course Haliburton doesn't want to let the Moon go," said Jarvis. "They'd like nothing more than to chop the Moon up into little pieces and sell it to Earthlings as moon rocks. And then they'd chop the Earth into pieces and sell it back to the Moon. That's just how evil they are."

The Terran public seems to agree. In a recent opinion poll, 58% of respondents agreed with the statement "Haliburton is an evil company," while 36% agreed with the statement that "Haliburton is an evil, fire-breathing lizard." 7% thought that Haliburton was "a small rodent indigenous to Guatemala, which subsists entirely on discarded cell phone batteries and coca beans." 76% said that they would buy Haliburton stock if they had the chance.

Jarvis and several dozen of her unemployed friends are coordinating another rally next week in Stockton. They are planning an aerial photo of the protesters, arranged in a crescent formation, simultaneously bearing their posteriors. The photo will be sent to the White House with the caption, "We've got your Moon right here!"

Meanwhile, the desolate Moon soldiers on, powerless to change course as it hurtles toward its inevitable doom.

A Crude Proposal

This, being the last day of twenty-diggety-six, is the day that the world turns its lonely eyes to me to solve one of the big outstanding problems of 2006. Yes, every year on this date I write down the ten biggest unresolved problems of the outgoing year on small pieces of paper and throw them in a hat. Then I put the hat on my head and dance around the house in my bathrobe to the strains of Journey's "Separate Ways" until all of the scraps fall out except for one. The last remaining problem is the one that I will solve, for the benefit of mankind. This year's big problems include global warming, the cancellation of *Arrested Development*, and that popping sound that my sternum is making these days when I move too suddenly. Most of the rest of the problems are related to some trouble spot in the world, such as Darfur, Afghanistan, or I-580 between Pleasanton and Livermore.

Having written down the world's biggest problems and placed them in a velvet fedora, I shall now proceed to dance gaily about my furniture and pets.

...

Whew! All of the problems have fallen out except one. I will now reach into the hat and reveal The Unresolved Problem of 2006 to be solved by me. And the winner is:

Iraq!

Wow, I was kind of hoping for that sternum thing, but rules are rules. Ok, so here's the deal:

Liberals are mad because they don't like the idea of a "war for oil." Liberals don't feel like they should have to fight for their oil, because they drive hybrid cars, which means that at worst they should have to play a rough game of ultimate Frisbee for oil, or maybe split the difference between making love and making war by having angry sex on the veranda for oil. Keep in mind they don't have a problem with wars per se; they would just rather talk about them over a nice latte at the U.N. rather than participate.

Conservatives are mad because they hate the idea of "nation building." They kind of like the "nation wrecking" bit, but "nation building" just blows. I mean, they hate it. They're all like, "Man, we hate nation building. It's just a bad idea all around. It never works out. I mean, hmm. Well, unless, maybe, just this once, we could.... I mean, it's not out of the realm of possibility that.... Oh. No. No, dammit! Oh man, now look what we've done. Geez. Man, I hate this nation building crap."

So here's what we do: Privatize the U.S. military. That's right, sell the whole thing off to the highest bidder.

You may object that such a solution is not "politically feasible." To this I respond: Did John F. Kennedy pause to ask whether his plan was 'politically feasible' before committing 400 American "advisors" in an unwinnable conflict in Southeast Asia? No sir, he did not! And yet, JFK is revered as a hero for his exploits as captain of PT-109, demonstrating that if you have to go on a trip with a Kennedy, the surest way to avoid drowning is, ironically, to travel by boat.

"Point taken," you say. "But what if some nutjob like Kim Jong Il or Tom Cruise buys it?"

"Nonsense," I say. The highest bidder is going to be (1) someone with more money than God; (2) someone who has a lot to gain by having a fleet of aircraft carriers and stealth bombers at their disposal; and (3) someone who has a lot to lose if the U.S. military falls into the hands of Kim Jong Il or Tom Cruise.

That's right, it's the oil companies. After all, if you're going to turn the military over to an oil company executive, it might as well be a *successful* oil company executive, right? So we let the oil companies take over the U.S. military and wage war at their discretion in order to secure a free flow of oil. We let them install a benevolent dictatorship in Iraq, and then move on to Iran and Syria if those dudes start causing problems. Maybe take care of that jackass in Venezuela too. And if there are any other trouble spots in the world that threaten the flow of oil, they'll handle those as well. Peace in the Sudan? Start some rumors about Jed Clampett finding "black gold" in his backyard in Darfur and the problem will be solved by this time tomorrow.

"What about the soldiers?" You say. "They didn't sign up to work for the oil companies!" No, they didn't. Which is why they'd be free to seek gainful employment elsewhere. The only way for the oil companies to keep their current personnel would be to pay them enough to make it worth their while. And maybe get them some friggin' body armor.

"But who's going to defend the U.S. if the oil companies are out conquering new oil fields?" you ask. Well, since the U.S. is the number one consumer of oil, I'm thinking the oil companies are going to try pretty hard to keep our economy on track. Which would include preventing things that disrupt the flow of oil, like big explosions and buildings falling over.

And best of all, it doesn't cost the U.S. taxpayer anything. In fact, we make money on the deal. I'm thinking we could get a couple of trillion bucks for the whole shebang. Maybe do it over eBay, and throw in free shipping and the CIA on one of those "Buy it now!" deals.

Oh, sure, the oil guys would get out of hand once in a while and maybe overthrow a democratic regime that was trying to nationalize its oil industry, but I think it would all even out. And on the occasion where they really made a mess of things, we'd be free to throw up our hands in exasperation along with the rest of the world. "Those greedy oil companies and their secret prisons and torture chambers," we'd say. "Man, if we didn't spend all our money on ridiculous social programs we'd totally start our own military and show those oil companies what's what." And then we'd go back to sipping our lattes and filling up our blood-and-oil hybrids.

So there you go. You're welcome. Maybe next year I'll get to that popping sound in my chest.

Undocumented Thoughts

Recently I was abducted by aliens. Or, to be politically correct, "undocumented beings." Alien is such a harsh and overly descriptive word. No need to hurt anyone's feelings, even if they do have six stomachs and plan to turn earth into a petting zoo.

I think it's admirable how the news media, flummoxed in their attempt to come up with a word describing people whose existence in this country is against the law, have seized upon undocumented as a reasonable approximation. It's the political equivalent of calling fat people "big-boned." Undocumented immigrant has become one of those cultural code phrases that sounds innocuous but actually hides an ugly reality, like "states' rights," "reproductive freedom," or "Rob Schneider comedy." Nor is the word undocumented limited to immigrants any more. I have to admit that I've resorted to using the term occasionally myself. My extensive MP3 collection, for example, is no longer comprised of "pirated songs," but rather "undocumented recordings." Just the other day a crate of undocumented cigarettes fell off a truck near my house. And that guy on the corner isn't a drug dealer, he's an undocumented pharmacist.

I do find it odd that a group of people who have received so much news coverage can remain "undocumented." I mean, when I see someone mowing a lawn on CNN, I consider them to be documented. It's like, dude, we got you on tape, ok? You're documented. I don't have that kind of documentation to prove that I'm doing my job. I have almost no evidence at all, to tell you the truth. Maybe *I'm* undocumented.

They've even done documentaries about undocumented immigrants. How is that possible? "Tonight: A documentary on undocumented immigrants, brought to you by the producer of 'A Spotlight on Shadows.'"

In California we had the inspired idea of giving undocumented immigrants driver's licenses. When people objected that this was a form of "back-door amnesty," proponents of the idea assured us that the driver's licenses would be distinguishable from regular driver's licenses, so that they could not legally be used for identification purposes. These driver's licenses would, in other words, be documented proof of being undocumented.

The proposal ran into trouble when it was pointed out that it's hard enough to drive on California's roads even without being legally required to be out of the country while doing it. Conservatives countered with a plan that would allow undocumented immigrants to remain in the country legally as long as they didn't leave their cars, but it died in committee. The issue was a political disaster for the governor, and Californians demonstrated their xenophobia en masse by electing a man who can't pronounce the name of the state.

Personally, I never understood the furor over the driver's license issue. I mean, when the state is already giving driver's licenses to millions of people who apparently don't know how to drive, it seems silly to complain about some of them not being able to read the street signs. I was all for the idea, although I have to admit that I assumed it was one of those deals where they send postcards out to criminals in the hopes that they'll show up to claim the yacht they've won. Congratulations, you've won a free trip to Mazatlan!

I don't want you to get the idea that I'm anti-immigrant. My grandparents were immigrants from Holland, as were my great-grandparents before them (we're an indecisive people). If I hated immigrants, then I would be a "self-hating Dutch person," which I'm pretty sure is redundant. Sorry if I'm coming off like Pat Buchanan on a bad day (or maybe Rob Schneider on a good day). I'm still a little sore from the undocumented prostate exam on the spacecraft.

May the Force Be with Me

I often hear people decrying what they refer to as "organized religion," and I can certainly empathize. Don't get me wrong; I do consider myself a religious person. On the other hand, I'm no advocate of organization. The solution to my plight would seem obvious, but I have as yet failed to locate a denomination that is sufficiently disorganized to meet my spiritual needs.

Certain charismatic sects are fairly disorganized and things can get a little out of hand at some of those black Baptist churches, but such mildly informal affairs are still a far cry from the unmitigated spiritual chaos for which my soul yearns. Why, for example, must we always go to church at 11am on Sunday morning? What's wrong with 2:37pm on the third Tuesday of every month whose name has a numerological value that is prime? And why the same rituals every time? Maybe some day we could play Hungry Hungry Hippos and beat each other with soup ladles rather than sing songs and pray. And what I wouldn't give to just once walk into a place of worship and have absolutely no idea who I'm going to be worshiping that morning. I'd be like, "Really? Kenny Rogers? Cool." And then I'd join the rest of the congregation in a stirring rendition of "Coward of the County." Or maybe I wouldn't. Because who's going to make me?

I've also heard that more wars are started over religion than anything else. This troubles me deeply, because I have not ONCE been asked to serve on our church's Religious Wars committee. I mean, I've probably played more Risk than just about any other member of our church. Does that count for nothing? I could advise them, for example, not to make Europe their power center because of all the borders you have to defend, and to avoid retreating to Australia unless you really want to spend the next three days on the losing end of a war of attrition. You might outlast the Presbyterians with that strategy, but you do NOT want to try that with Jesuits or Shiite Muslims.

No, instead I have to serve on committees that are concerned with unbelievably dull things like making sure needy people have adequate food, shelter and medical care. Occasionally I make a motion to start a war, and I just get blank stares. Last time I moved that we declare war on the Quakers. They're *pacifists*, for crying out loud. We could kick their asses, confiscate their oats, and be home before dark. But nobody would even second the motion. I don't get it. What's the point of being religious if we're not going to start any wars?

Disorganized people don't start wars. Well, occasionally they start them, but they never finish them. Frankly, disorganized people don't finish much of anything. It's part of their charm. Hell, sometimes they'll start a thought

If we were to eliminate organized religion, we would eliminate the number one cause of war. Of course, we'd still have the number two cause, which would then become number one. I wonder what that would be? Land? Food? Oil? The desire for power? Freedom? I'd say we should probably eliminate them all to be on the safe side.

It surprises me how few wars are fought in the name of evil. I think Darth Vader is the only one who ever stood up and said, "Hey, we're going to be the bad guys in this war. Oppression, cruelty, suffering, that's us. I'm going to hire gaunt lieutenants with clipped British accents, put the word 'Death' in the name of our headquarters, blow up peaceful planets for giggles, and wear an outfit that would make Satan shit his pants. Who wants in?"

Using the Dark Side of the Force must have about the same effect as eating

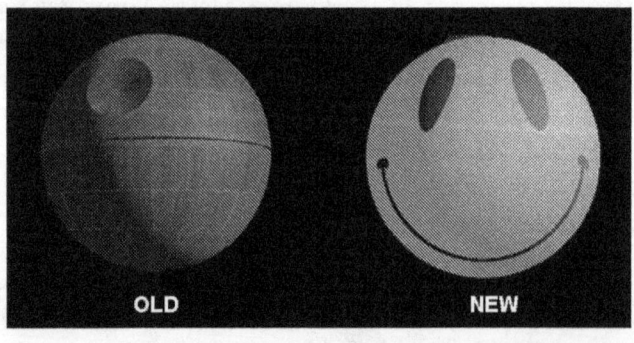

paint chips, because those guys were none too bright. If I were the Empire's marketing director, I'd have made a few little changes that would have gone a long way toward improving their image:

OLD	NEW
Galactic Empire	Democratic Federation of Free Planets
Storm Troopers	Customer Service Representatives
Star Destroyer	Nuclear Fusion Cleanup Vehicle
Dark Side of the Force	Look! Ewoks!
Death Star	Moon o' Fun
TIE Fighter	TIE Fighter (What, it's just not very threatening-sounding)

In fact, if you were really clever, you could probably find a way to convince people that the Dark Side of the Force was really the Light Side, and vice versa. You'd use the language of the Jedi order to promote your own nefarious purposes, and people would get confused and not know which side to support. And the really great thing is, even if you lost the war, you'd have convinced a lot of simple-minded people that Dark = Light and Light = Dark and that these Jedi bastards are just a bunch of troublemakers.

Nothing of that sort is likely to happen here on earth, where the world's religions continue to cause untold problems. Sadly, I think I'm about to give up my quest for a truly disorganized religion. The problem is that as soon as you involve other people, you have to start worrying about schedules and doctrines and people who refuse to see things your way no matter how hard you explain it to them. In the end, my religion is nobody's business but mine and God's – and He'd better watch it, or it's going to be just me pretty damn quick.

Belgium: France Keeps Touching Me

In an incident that threatens to upset the delicate balance of power in Europe's metaphorical backseat, Belgium has once again accused France of unwanted touching.

The site of the alleged touching is an area surrounding the Meuse River, just west of Luxembourg. At a press conference on Tuesday, Belgian Foreign Minister Hans Phillipe showed satellite photos which he insisted "show clearly that France is poking Belgium."

France's ambassador to Belgium, Jean-Marie St. Claude characterized Belgium's claims as "ridiculous." In a written statement, he said that France was clearly on its side of the Franco-Belgian border.

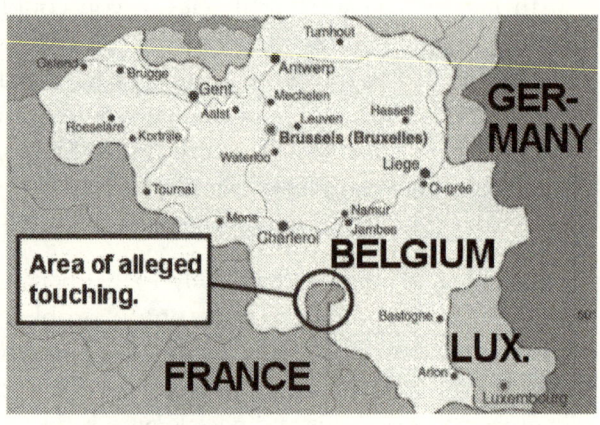

The other two Benelux countries, who asked to remain anonymous, were supportive of Belgium. "This isn't the first time that France has stuck its finger where it isn't wanted," one of the countries said. The other one offered, "I don't think that's a finger." Western Europe responded with a collective "ewwww" and demanded that Paris clean up its act.

The incident immediately set off an outcry in the United States that Paris be sent back to jail where she belongs.

6

Fiction and Unabashed Hyperbole

Wherein any pretense of coherency is abandoned.

For some reason, I always thought I was some day going to be a Serious Writer. I love sci fi, and I've written several sci fi short stories. You won't find any of them posted or published anywhere, though, because they pretty much suck. I've got the rejection letters from a number of prestigious sci fi magazines (ha!) to prove it. It's only recently that I began to write humor seriously (and if you don't think you can write humor seriously, you should see the joke that my non-humor writing was).

Here's the problem: I don't have the attention span to write serious fiction. I get bored with my characters and settings, and keep coming up with crazy new ideas that I want to incorporate. My characters start to question why they're stuck it such dull, preposterous situations, and refuse to do what I want them to do. They crack jokes at inappropriate times, and their grave predicaments are undercut by my inability to provide straight exposition without irony.

At some point I gave up trying to write serious fiction and gave in to my urge to write rambling, semi-coherent nonsense. You've probably figured that out by now, unless you just happened to pick up this book and turn to this page (in which case, how weird is it that you just happened to turn to this page? Boo! Freaked you out a little, didn't I?).

These days it's rare that I'll set out to write a "story," but occasionally one will sort of accidentally emerge, like when you start making a peanut butter and jelly sandwich and you notice that the smear of peanut butter looks like the Virgin Mary and then you can't eat the sandwich until your cat jumps on the counter and licks it until it turns into Axl Rose. And then you still can't eat it because, eww, Axl Rose.

So, as the title indicates, this chapter is filled with stuff that mostly didn't really happen. To call these posts "fiction" is probably a little generous. Most of them started out with some basis in fact, but about halfway through the first sentence I got bored with reality and start making up absurd nonsense to spice things up a bit. Sometimes I didn't even make it that far, as in "The Legend of Diesel." "The Legend of Diesel" was a deliberate attempt to explain my nickname in a way that was so ridiculous and out of character for me that no one would believe a word of it. It is, after all, a ridiculous nickname that doesn't fit me at all, so I thought it only fitting that there be a suitably incredible explanation for it.

I Do Mind! I Do!

Recently my family went out to eat at a local Mexican restaurant, and the hostess asked if we minded being seated "in the back." The way she said "in the back" made me think that perhaps we would have to crawl through a drainage pipe to get there, but being the agreeable sort that I am, I reflexively said, "That's fine."

"Mind if I seat you in the back?"

I regretted it immediately. While we waited, I speculated as to what horrors would confront us "in the back." Would there be chairs? Tables? Exposed wiring hanging from rusted nails? Perhaps we would be expected to scavenge our own appetizers from the dumpster behind the meat-packing plant. I looked around for other diners headed for 'the back,' anxious to form an alliance to ensure the safety of our guacamole supply.

"We should never have agreed to sit 'in the back,'" I said to my wife. "Now we have no one to blame but ourselves." There would be no point in complaining once we were back there.

"You say you don't mind," the waiter would snarl, befuddled and a bit put out. "Why do you say you don't mind, if you *do* mind?"

Why indeed? I would have no answer for that. And there we would sit, tossing tortilla chips at rabid monkeys and trying to build a table out of cardboard and packing foam.

As the hostess came for us I wanted to say something, *anything*, to get out of my commitment to sit "in the back." But what? It's not like she was unclear about what she was asking me. They ask you that question for a reason: Because most people *do* mind sitting in the back. They mind it one hell of a lot, to tell you the truth. But some people – maybe they're a little crazy, maybe they have a death wish – some people *don't* mind. And there's no switching sides. You don't suddenly go from being someone who *doesn't* mind to being someone who *does* mind, just like that.

What kind of explanation could I offer for my sudden conversion? A minute ago I was all, "Screw my family's safety! I want to be Mr. Tough Guy, hanging out 'in the back' with the crack whores and guacamole pirates!" And then just like that I develop an overwhelming need to sit somewhere with modern sanitation facilities and fresh salsa? No, that wouldn't fly. The fronters would never accept us. We'd always be the Table that Thought They Could Make It In the Back But Then Chickened Out.

We took a collective deep breath and headed toward the back. The fronters averted their eyes as we walked by. We passed the bar, the kitchen, the bathrooms... and kept going. As the bright light of the restaurant's main dining room grew ever dimmer, I silently whispered a prayer for protection against the hazards and travails we would soon face. Before I knew it, we were there.

It turns out that "the back" was a lot like "the front," but slightly further away. Hence the name, I suppose. I had the enchiladas.

Mixed Fruits and Metaphors

EXT. GARDEN OF EDEN. DAY.

Adam is busily scribbling on a piece of paper with a pencil when God quietly walks up beside him.

God: Hey Adam, what's up?

Adam: Oh, uh... hey, there, God. I was just, you know, coming up with some more animal names.

God: I thought you named all the animals already.

Adam: The Mediterranean animals, yeah. But I figure that you've got a lot of animals in other climates that still need names.

God: What's a "polar bear"?

Adam: Geez, I don't know. A bear that like poles? You don't have to use it if you don't want.

God: No, no, it's a good name. I'll come up with something. Ooh, I like this one. *Kangaroo*. Sounds like something you could put in your pocket. Speaking of which, I noticed you're wearing trousers stitched together from leaves.

Adam: Oh, that. Yeah, I was feeling a little self-conscious with all my, you know, parts hanging out.

God: Did you eat from that tree I told you not to eat from?

Adam: Ummmm... Actually that was the woman.

God: The woman? You mean Eve?

Adam: No, the other woman. Of course Eve.

God: Don't get smart with me, mister. You've got a lot more ribs.

Adam: Ok, sorry. Anyway, Eve said the snake told her it was ok....

God: The *snake*? Eve is listening to *snakes* now?

Adam: She goes a little crazy for a few days around this time of the month.

God: Man, I knew talking animals were a mistake.

Adam: You mean the animals really can talk? I thought Eve had gotten into the happy mushrooms again.

God: That's it, no more talking animals. Also, the snake is going to have to crawl around on its belly from now on.

Adam: As opposed to...?

God: Well, walking on its legs, of course.

Adam: Snakes don't have legs.

God: Of course they do. Four stubby little legs.

Adam: You're thinking of a lizard.

God: No, I'm pretty sure it's a snake.

Adam: No, the ones with legs are called lizards. Remember, you wanted to call them all "snakes" but I said that I thought we needed a different name for the ones with legs. So I came up with "lizards."

God: Oh yeah. It's too bad in a way.

Adam: What?

God: I was really looking forward to pulling its legs off.

Adam: Maybe just remove the wings?

God: Yeah, that'll learn it. No more winged snakes. Oh, and one more thing: I have to kick you out of the garden.

Adam: Oh. Because of the fruit thing?

God: Yeah. Rules are rules.

Adam: Ok. It was getting kind of dull in here anyway. What's it like out there?

God: To be honest, most of it is kind of crummy compared to this.

Adam: What? Why? Didn't you create everything perfect?

God: Inside the garden, yes. Outside... not so much. And now that you've sinned, you have to go out there.

Adam: Wait a minute. You deliberately created a shitty world all around this garden so that just in case we screwed up you'd have a place to exile us to? Nice.

God: No, it didn't get screwed up until you ate the fruit.

Adam: Wha...? I took one little bite of a piece of fruit and I screwed up the *entire world*? This doesn't make any sense. Things look fine to me.

God: Inside the garden, yes. But not out there.

Adam: But shouldn't the garden be the place that got screwed up? Does the screw-up radiation just skip right over the garden?

God: Er, no, the garden will start to go to pot pretty quick too.

Adam: So why can't we just stay here?

God: Well, there's also the matter of the Tree of Life.

Adam: Tree of Life? So there are two magic trees in the garden? I thought there was only the Tree of the Knowledge of Good and Not So Good.

God: Evil. It's called evil. You can stop pretending that you don't know what it's called.

Adam: Evil, huh? It's got sort of a wicked sound to it.

God: Yeah, so there's also the Tree of Life. It's the one on the other side of the tool shed.

Adam: Really? I thought that was an apricot tree.

God: No, it's the Tree of Life. And I can't have you eating from it, because then you'll live forever. Which sounds like a good thing, but now that you've been corrupted you're going to have to die.

Adam: But I've already eaten some of that fruit.

God: Yeah, but not after you ate the fruit of the Tree of the Knowledge of Good and Evil. Eating from the TOKOGE counteracts the effects of the Tree of Life. But if you eat from the Tree of Life *after* eating from the TOKOGE, you'll be evil and live forever.

"Nice snake. Metaphorically speaking, of course."

Adam: What kind of twisted mind comes up with this stuff? Are there any other magic trees I should know about? Maybe one that'll make me shit diamonds?

God: Look, don't make this any more difficult than it has to be. Ok, here comes Eve. When she gets here, tell her you want to go for a walk and head down that path to the gate. The angel with the fiery sword will see you out.

Adam: "See us out"?

God: He's going to guard the gate to the garden so you don't get any ideas about coming back for your couch or anything.

Adam: Is there going to be a wall around the garden?

God: Of course.

Adam: Is anybody going to be going in or out after we leave?

God: No.

Adam: Then why do you need a gate?

God: Ok, enough questions. Mysterious ways and all that. Just leave quietly, ok? Don't make a scene.

Adam: This sucks.

God: Hey, I told you not to eat the fruit.

Adam: Here's an idea: Next time, build the wall around the Forbidden Tree. I mean, what the hell is up with the cobblestone path and park benches?

God: I thought it made a nice sitting area.

Adam: Well it would have if the Fruit of Evil wasn't hanging over our heads!

God: Ok, here's the deal. I'm going to tell you something that might freak you out a little, but hopefully things will start to make a little more sense to you.

Adam: Um, ok.

God: A lot of times when I say an "angel" is going to be doing this or that, it's not literally an angel. Sometimes the phrase "the angel of the Lord" just means me. But primitive minds have a hard time comprehending someone doing so many things in so many different places at once.

Adam: So... you're not really sending an angel to guard the garden?

God: It depends what you mean by "really." Maybe you should come up with another word for when we're going to use concrete terms to refer to abstractions like good and evil and sin and heaven and grace and perfection.

Adam: Hmmm. How about "metaphorical?"

God: Excellent!

Adam: So you'll be putting a metaphorical angel in front of the gate?

God: The metaphorical gate, yes.

Adam: Are the trees metaphorical?

God: It kind of sounds like it, doesn't it? If they weren't, this whole garden scene wouldn't make a lot of sense.

Adam: So maybe the entire garden is....

God: Yes, yes. Now you're starting to see why I thought this would freak you out. Just keep in mind that none of this is any less "real" just because it's metaphorical. You just have to remember not to push the metaphor too far, or the whole thing starts to sound absurd.

Adam: So Eve and I....

Eve: Hey guys, what's the deal with the angel at the gate?

God: He's here to escort you out of the garden.

Eve: He's what?!

God: Adam will explain everything.

A Slurry of Monsters

As my wife and I were walking through our almond orchard the other day, inspecting the trees for blight, rust and urban sprawl, I caught a glimpse of a distant gathering of undead creatures. At first I thought they were zombies, but they could have been ghouls. They're hard to tell apart at a distance.

Our orchard was planted on top of an Indian burial ground, so it's not uncommon for us to see various flavors of undead roaming amongst the trees in search of human flesh and a place to whizz. Well, technically it isn't so much a burial ground as it is a casino that collapsed due to God's punishment on immorality and a lack of sufficient sheer support. Efforts were made to rescue the trapped gamblers, but when their relatives were informed that the odds of anyone getting out alive were a million to one, they decided to take their chances elsewhere.

So now our orchard is plagued by the spirits and/or reanimated corpses of several hundred dead gamblers still trying to beat the odds.

I grabbed my wife's arm and whispered, "Look! A bunch of zombies!"

"A bunch of zombies?" She said disdainfully, barely glancing in the direction I pointed.

"Yeah, look! I think they're grazing...or something."

"I'm pretty sure it's not a 'bunch' of zombies," she said. "And zombies don't graze; they scavenge for carrion."

"What do you mean, it's not a bunch of zombies? There are like eight of them."

"No, I mean it's not called a 'bunch.' You know how it's a pride of lions, a parliament of owls, a murder of crows...."

"A trifling of meerkats," I added helpfully.

"In any case, I think those are ghouls. They're not scavenging; they're menacing. Zombies scavenge; ghouls menace."

"That doesn't sound right," I said.

"Ok, you're the expert. It's not like I'm a fourth grade teacher or anything."

"Ok, ok," I said. "So what do you call a group of zombies?"

She thought for a moment. "A groan, I think."

"A groan of zombies? You're making that up."

"It's a groan of zombies and a chilling of ghouls. I think that's right."

"What about skeletons?"

"A rattle of skeletons."

"Poltergeists?"

"An annoyance of poltergeists."

"Mummies?"

"Tangle."

"Vampires?"

"Fang."

I thought for a while, trying to stump her. My wife's knowledge of the undead and cryptozoology is formidable. Finally I seized on one that I was sure she wouldn't know.

"What about sasquatches?" I said. "Tell me what a group of sasquatches is called, smarty pants."

She sighed and looked bored. "A blur of sasquatches," she said.

Damn, she's good, I thought.

"We should go," she said. "They look like they're menacing in this direction."

"Hey," I said, as they shambled closer. "I think that's just a bunch of drunk teenagers."

"A posse of drunk teenagers," she corrected.

"Still, they're menacing in this direction."

"Yes they are."

"How do you kill drunken teenagers again?" I asked. We didn't get many of those around here.

"Bullet to the brain," She said.

"Thank God," I said. "Beheading is a bitch."

We drew our sidearms and fired.

What I Learned This Morning from a Sea Turtle

I was accosted this morning by a large sea turtle. I had arisen early to steal the neighbor's newspaper (I cancelled my subscription when I learned the editor was a freethinker and a bigamist), and just as I stepped outside, I saw it. The turtle must have been a good 5 feet long and 3.5 feet wide (these are shell measurements), and I would estimate that it weighed at least 200 pounds. I certainly couldn't lift him, and I'm hella strong. I attribute my exceptional strength to a daily regimen of vitamins and backgammon, although I'm also 1/32 Apache Indian, so that's sort of an X factor.

It's hard to say what the turtle wanted. He insisted that I relate his demands to the world in Cantonese, and my accent isn't so good. Frankly, I had some difficulty understanding him as well. At first I thought he wanted all the tops to my old cereal boxes, but upon retrospection that may have been due to some baseless preconceptions on my part. It's really not fair to make generalizations about all sea turtles based on a single previous experience.

Having learned my lesson about stereotyping and intolerance, I shot him. I abhor violence, except when it comes to large things I fear and don't understand. I guess I'll never know what he wanted. Maybe just a chance to live out his dreams, to laugh, to fall in love, to experience new things, to see if he could hold his breath longer than all the other sea turtles in his class to impress some girl sea turtle who is busy talking on her cell phone and putting on nail polish at a green light with like sixteen other sea turtles honking their horns behind her. Who can say?

I buried him in the backyard with all my old cereal box tops, just in case.

Imagine My Surprise

I've always been a shy, introspective sort. I had a hard time making friends as a kid, so I resorted to devising imaginary friends. Fortunately, I was quite imaginative and was able to construct entirely believable fictional characters with whom to while away recesses.

My best friend was Toby. Toby was everything you might want in a friend: generous, helpful, and just a fun guy to be around in general. He was athletic but he didn't rub your face in it, and he was a good student but not a brown noser. He was smart enough to stay out of trouble but mischievous enough to engage in the occasional prank. He was, as far as I could imagine, the best possible friend.

Things were going well with me and Toby. Too well, in fact.

As I mentioned, I was an introspective and creative child. I was the kind of kid who could never just let things be. I drove my teachers insane with my incessant questions. I was always asking "why?"

It was not surprising, then, that I soon started to wonder why Toby was hanging around with me. Surely a kid like Toby had his pick of friends. Why me? I was unathletic, shy, unpopular and frankly a little odd. What did Toby see in me?

Soon flaws began to appear in Toby's character. I came to suspect that he spent time with me primarily out of some sense of obligation. This became clear to me over dinner one night at Toby's house. Toby's family was very wealthy, occupying a vast hidden mansion in the woods behind my family's modest ranch house. I often went over there for dinner, because his mom made fantastic lasagna and they had a trampoline.

Toby's dad was a minister and was always talking about helping "the less fortunate." He let something slip that night that about how proud he was of Toby for "doing his part." He quickly changed the subject, but it was clear that he was talking about me. I was "the less fortunate." Not because I was poor or handicapped or something, but because I was me.

After that, things were different between me and Toby. The spell had been broken. Toby started hanging out with the more popular kids. He played basketball with them during recess. He would always ask me if I wanted to play, but he knew I would say no. I'd rather be alone than embarrass myself on the basketball court.

Then Toby got a girlfriend. Her name was Angela, and she was the most popular girl in school. They were too young to date, *per se*, but they spent as much time they could together. Toby was always mysteriously "out" when I called. Eventually I stopped calling.

Toby got Angela pregnant during freshman year of high school. They moved to Alaska, where Toby's uncle got him a job gutting fish. I heard that Angela divorced him eight months after the baby was born. She and their daughter moved in with her parents in Michigan.

Toby called me three weeks ago. He said he was in Sacramento, and asked if I wanted to meet him. I drove up there and met him at Denny's. He had a beer gut and was losing his hair. He said he was working odd jobs, trying to get up enough money to start a landscaping business, but it was hard because his rent was so high. It turned out he had been living at a Motel 6 for three months.

I told him I had a finished room in my barn he could stay in if he wanted to. I had been thinking of putting in a bathroom, and asked if he wanted to help out with the project in exchange for room and board. He protested that he couldn't possibly impose on me, but not very convincingly. We swung by the motel, picked up his meager belongings, and headed back to Ripon.

Toby lives in my barn. He's a loser now, like me.

How the Almond Farmer Saved Christmas

During the 2005-06 cropyear, more than $1.3 million worth of almonds were stolen from growers and shippers in the San Joaquin Valley. Truckload after truckload, thieves allegedly trespassed onto properties, cut fences and broke locks to get to the valuable nuts. Sheriff's deputies say thieves hot-wired several tractor-trailers around the Central Valley and were able to flee with almonds that were awaiting shipment overseas.

The Thule fog whipped around Santa's sleigh, obscuring his vision of the ground below. "On Donner! On Blitzen! We're going to be late!" Not for the first time he cursed himself for letting Rudolph go. The old boy had been hitting the nog pretty hard lately, but his incandescent schnoz sure would have come in handy on a night like this.

A loud crack and the howls of terrified reindeer broke the calm of the still winter air. "Up! Pull up!" Santa barked. But it was too late. The reindeer flew headlong through a tangled mess of knotty tree branches. Santa gritted his teeth as the branches whipped past, smacking his face and tearing the buttons off his coat. Finally the rig came to a halt, the reindeers' antlers hopelessly entangled in the branches, the sleigh dangling precariously beneath them. The ground could be five feet or fifty feet down. It was impossible to tell in the fog. "Blasted cartographer elves!" Santa spat, as the sleigh rocked nauseatingly. Where his charts showed an empty field he had found an orchard. Reindeer bleated pathetically above him and Santa tried to stand to appraise the situation. He lost his balance and flailed about, finally grasping the end of a branch. It was leafless and dead looking, with only the hint of new buds tucked away under the coarse grayish brown bark. A few tiny blackened bits of fruit dangled from the end. "Not supposed to be an orchard here," Santa muttered. "And it could at least be chestnuts. These look like...."

"Almonds," said a gruff voice below. Except he pronounced it A-munds, so it rhymed with salmon. Judging from the voice, Santa figured he was only about ten feet up.

"Al-monds, you mean," said Santa. "Who is that?"

"Name's Jess Van Den Berg," said the man. "I'm an a-mund farmer. And no, I don't mean al-mond. You're in Ripon, California. We're the a-mund capitol of the world. And we call them a-munds."

"Ok, fine," said Santa. "I'm in a bit of a hurry. This is my big night, you know. Lots of presents to deliver. Do you think you could help me out of these trees?"

"Sure," said Jess. "I'll get my chainsaw and a ladder. One thing, though...."

"What is it?" Santa asked, impatiently. The reindeer continued to flail about and make plaintive sounds.

Jess continued, "There was a big a-mund theft out here recently. I lost about half of my crop. It's not going to be much of a Christmas for my family."

"Uh huh," said Santa.

"And well, you're Santa Claus, so you can pretty much give anything to anybody, right?"

"Within reason," Santa said cautiously.

"Ok, well I was hoping you could get me my nuts back."

"Uhh...."

"Or not, whatever. In any case, I should probably see if there are any sleighs caught in the trees of my walnut orchard across the levee."

"Ok, ok! You can have your nuts back."

"Really? That's fantastic! Ok, wait right here. I'm going to get my chainsaw."

Jess hopped in his pickup and sped back to the barn where he kept his equipment. He was thrilled. This was going to be the best Christmas ever. He couldn't wait to get home and tell the family how he saved Christmas and got his nuts back.

He grabbed his chainsaw, fifty feet of rope and a long extension ladder, threw them in the back of the pickup, and drove back out to where Santa's sleigh still hung pathetically in the trees. It took him nearly an hour, but he managed to work the reindeer loose and lowered the whole rig to the ground without so much as a broken antler. He was sweaty and his muscles twitched with exhaustion, but he had done it. He had saved Christmas.

Standing there next to Santa's sleigh piled high with presents meant for good little boys and girls across the globe, he felt a strange sensation, a combination of pride that he had something to do with the spreading of such joy, and embarrassment that he had put his own nuts ahead of the happiness of all those children. It was a humbling experience.

Santa put his hand on Jess' shoulder. "Jess, I can't tell you how grateful I am for your help. There are going to be a lot of little boys and girls who are going to be very happy tomorrow morning, thanks to you."

Jess smiled sheepishly, thinking back to the joyful Christmas mornings of his youth. Tears began to well up in his eyes.

Santa hopped back into the sleigh, then looked back, with a twinkle in his eye. "I suppose you know now, Jess, that your nuts were in your heart all along."

Jess nodded slowly and smiled as Santa grabbed the reigns. Then a confused look came over his face.

"My what?" Jess said.

"Your nuts," Santa said flatly. "They're in your –"

Jess spat and shook his head. "Look, maybe that kind of crap flies at the North Pole, but here in Ripon we pay our debts. And you owe me twenty tons of nuts. I can't believe you're trying to screw the guy who saved Christmas out of his nuts."

Santa said, "You see, Jess, I said what I had to say to complete my mission, but I don't make the rules. The fact is, you've been rather naughty this year...."

"Naughty?! I friggin' saved Christmas!"

"Yes," Santa said. "That will factor positively in next year's accounting, I'm sure. However, you used a lot of Malathion for fumigation this year. Do you know how bad that stuff is for the environment? And I believe there were a few instances where you threw construction waste in your burn pile this past summer. Very naughty, Jess."

"Unbelievable," Jess said. He stepped in front of the sleigh. "Ok, I think I know how to settle this," he said.

"Jess, get out of the way. I've got a lot of presents to deliver."

"I didn't want to have to do this, Santa. But here's the deal: I've got a chainsaw. You don't. Give me my nuts or yours are going back up in that tree."

Santa sputtered and cursed, but finally gave in. He reached into his sleigh and hauled out a small bag, no larger than Jess' fist. He tossed it to Jess.

Jess held the bag upside down, thinking Santa was making fun of him. To his surprise, a great cascade of almonds poured out of the bag. And they kept pouring out, until there was a pile up to Jess's waist. Finally he closed up the bag, convinced that Santa had made good on the deal.

"They're all there," Santa said. "Twenty tons."

"Good," Jess said.

"Are all of you almond farmers this stubborn?" Santa asked.

Jess grinned. "Pretty much," he said. "And it's a-munds."

"But there's an L in it," Santa protested. "It's *all*-monds."

"Sure, there's an L when you spell it, but when you say the word, there's no L."

Santa sighed in resignation, as the reindeer took flight. "No L?" He shouted back to Jess.

"No L!" Jess shouted back.

And the words echoed in Santa's head as he flew over the little town of Ripon, reflecting on what he had learned about keeping Christmas promises.

Noel, Noel,

Noel, Noel,

Born is the King of Israel.

The Legend of Diesel

There wasn't much to do in the tiny West Texas town I grew up in 'cept throw rocks at crows and rip off car stereos, so I was bound to get busted for the second one eventually. At the time I was runnin' with a couple of other no-good dead-enders, who went by the names Skeet and Colt. "Skeet" because his daddy was always shootin' at him, and "Colt" because he kicked so hard that his momma died two months before he was born. Me? Hell, nobody even thought I deserved a name. They all just called me "kid," usually with a "good-for-nothing" in front of it. Skeet and Colt were sixteen. I was only fifteen, but they let me run with them cuz I was good in a fight and could out-smoke and out-drink the both of them combined.

So after they busted us we got hauled before the judge, all dressed in our Sunday best. The judge was probably just gonna send us to the juvie camp, cuz that's what they do around there to kids what ain't got no future. But then our no-good fat-ass public defender opens his pie hole and says, "Yer honor, these is just three messed up kids." He meant it to be helpful, but wouldn't you know that right then and there was when I got all fed up to here being called *kid*, so I says to the judge, "Yer honor, I ain't no *kid*." Which is how Skeet and Colt got sent to the juvie camp, but me, the youngest one, got seven years hard labor.

I ain't gonna lie to you, that work farm wasn't no fun. We spent fourteen hours a day breakin' rocks with picks. They didn't tell us why, and we didn't ask. We ain't never seen anybody pick up any of them rocks we broke, so we figgered we was breakin' rocks to build character or some such nonsense. Well, my character got built into a mean-ass sonofobitch with hands like leather and arms like steel cables. The guards was hard on us, but the way the Texas sun beat down on us there weren't no question whose bitches we really was.

They labeled me "uncooperative" on account of that's what I was. The other convicts took a break every couple hours to have a cigarette, but not me, cuz to have a cigarette you had to say "Please boss can I get a light?" and I wasn't please-bossin' nobody. I went for six months without a cigarette, which was tough, cuz I started smoking when I was four. Then one day it got so hot that an old dead oak tree caught on fire, and I ran right over there and lit my cigarette. The other convicts was mighty upset that the one shade tree for a hundred miles around got burnt down, but I was happy as a pig in shit to get a light that I didn't have to please-boss for. I chain-smoked from that one cigarette for the next six and a half years, and never once had to ask for a light.

Once I had my cigarette goin', them other convicts expected I was gonna join them for their breaks, but my daddy always told me not to fraternize with no-good reprobates, cuz that's how he became one. Well I shore as hell wasn't gonna turn into a no-good reprobate like my daddy, so I just kept on breakin' rocks and chain smokin' while they was chattin' up the guards at their purdy little ten minute convict picnic. Only reason I ever came over there was to fill up my drinkin' bottle from the big water tank on the back of the prison truck. The water tasted like iron and pesticides, but I figured I was gettin' my minerals and keepin' my insides clean of bugs, so I didn't mind.

This went on for awhile, but pretty soon the other convicts got sick of me actin' like I was better than they was, and breakin' six times as much rocks as they was breakin', and the guards were itchin' for a please-boss, cuz please-bosses are what prison guards get instead of the love of a good woman. So they was makin' fun of me and callin' me a bitch for workin' through my break, and then somebody says, "Man, he must have gasoline in that bottle, the way he's workin.'" And then another guy, the biggest, meanest guy in the place, who they called Tex on account of he was from Oklahoma, spoke up. He says, "Naw, the way he smokes, he's a diesel engine." And then they started callin' me *Diesel*, and saying, "Hey Diesel, come get some more fuel" and dumbass shit like that. When I just kept breaking rocks, they says to the guard, "Boss, make him come over here." Boss didn't want to, but then they started sayin', "I bet you couldn't get old Diesel to come over here if you tried." And Boss didn't like that. They kept on him until finally he says, "Boy, get yer ass over here." And he put a period on it by spittin' his Skoal juice in my direction.

Well I figured I was there to break rocks, not to entertain Boss and the no-good reprobates, so that's what I kept doin.' Boss told me two more times, but I just kept on breakin' rocks. Finally he says to the no-good reprobates, "You grab that sorry sumbitch and bring him over here." And it took eight of them, but that's what they did. I fought like a wildcat, but Tex socked me good in the gut, and I went down. The rest of them piled on, and pretty quick I was flatter on the ground than roadkill. Somehow I still had my cigarette in my mouth, and Boss came over and plucked it out with his soft little pudgy fingertips.

Boss was one sorry excuse for a man. He used to tell us how he'd punish his dog when he misbehaved by whuppin' him till he bled, and then tyin' him to a tree and puttin' hamburger patties out on the ground just out of the dog's reach, so the poor mutt would spend all day cuttin' up his neck just to get a sniff of that meat. It wasn't long after the day I got named Diesel that we heard that Boss's wife left him for a ballet dancer, and he had to quit because he couldn't get no respect any more from the convicts. Even a pansy-ass ballet dancer was more of a man than him, the convicts would say.

But we didn't know about the dancing fruit that day he got the convicts to hold me down and he plucked the cigarette from my mouth. After that he spat a big wad of chaw juice in my face, which was bad enough, but what he did next marked the both of us for life. He ripped my shirt open and started burnin' me with that cigarette. It hurt so bad I didn't notice what he was doin' at first, but then I saw that we was making letters. That must have been the slowest burnin' cigarette in the history of Injun tobacco, cuz it felt like it took him an hour to burn *D-E-S-E-L* into my skin. It smelled like hamburgers, and made me think of Boss's sorry-ass dog. No dog deserves to be treated like that, I thought. And right then and there I swore some day Boss was going to know what it felt like to be hamburger.

After he was done burnin' me, he flicked the cigarette away and the convicts let me go. I just lay there for a spell, restin' up and smellin' the hamburger smell. If they figgered I didn't have no fight left in me, boy was they wrong. I got to my feet, brushed myself off, then laid the biggest haymaker you ever seen across Tex's jaw. There was a *POP!* that they must have heard in El Paso, and Tex fell to his knees, his jaw hangin' down three inches farther than the Almighty intended, so he looked like one sorry-ass dumbfounded okie, which is what he was.

Then, while the rest of them were still standin' there doin' their best impressions of a dumbfounded okie with a busted jaw, I reached down and picked up my cigarette, which still had about a quarter inch of life in it, took another cigarette from the pack in my sleeve and lit it from the dying butt. I got a real nice cherry goin' on it and then planted that red hot tip on my chest, right between the *D* and the *E*. When I had torched a real purdy letter *I*, I took a nice long drag and said, "*I* before *E*, shitheads." Then I went back to breakin' rocks. Nobody laid a finger on me after that, and six and a half years of rock-breakin' later, I was a free man.

First thing I did when I got out was look up that sorry-ass pudgy-fingered prison guard, who wasn't a prison guard no more on account of gettin' his ass fired for havin' a cheatin' whore ballet-dancer-lover for a wife. He lived in a dirty old trailer that smelled like onions and sweaty feet. When

I came by, he was up to his old tricks, teasin' his mutt with hamburger. The dog was chained up to a tree out back, and a nice big pancake of ground beef lay on the dirt just out of his reach. Boss was sittin' there in a lawn chair, drinkin' a Blue Ribbon and laughin' at the poor starving mutt. That dog was the ugliest damn creature God ever put on this planet, and I ain't entirely sure God's the one what did it. He looked like he was half Doberman, half Rottweiler, and half demon from the pit of hell, cuz that's just how big and mean he was. Boss had drawn a line that marked how far the dog could get from the tree, so he could tease him all he wanted without gettin' bit. Boss kept sayin', "Come 'n' get it, Duke! Come and get it!" And all I could think of is what kind of sorry ass pansy you have to be to give your dog a fag name like Duke. When Duke got too close, Boss would spit a wad of Skoal juice in his eyes.

I was about to walk up and give that jackass what-for when a phone rang and he high-tailed it back into his trailer. I strolled right up to the demon-mutt, picked up the hamburger patty he'd probably been eyein' since last Tuesday, and tossed it where he could reach it. The dog gave me no mind and went to work on that meat. I had just enough time to scrub out that line Boss had drawn and make another one with my boot. Then I went back and sat down under a tree, where I'd have a good view of the show.

Soon enough Boss came back out the trailer and got back to his fun. He pulled his lawn chair up to the line I'd drawn and said, "Dammit, Duke, you better not've ate my hamburger!" Now I know dogs can't smile, but I swear that demon dog looked over at me for a split second and gave me the evillest fang-filled grin you ever saw. Then he launched hisself toward that sorry-ass dipshit and sunk about sixty of those teeth into the right side of Boss's face. Boss screamed like a little bitch, but that dog held on like it was the one thing he was put on earth for. Finally he ripped half the meat off Boss's face like chicken from a bone, and Boss fell back on his lawn chair, sobbing and trying to hold on what was left of his face.

That's when I walked up and threw another hamburger patty to the dog. He dropped Boss's cheek and gobbled up the hamburger. I picked up the bloody chunk of flesh and tossed it at Boss. "You're lucky your face tastes as bad as that shit you chew," I said.

Boss looked at me with the same look he probably used when he walked in on his wife gettin' friendly with the candy-ass dancer. "You...?" was all he could muster.

"Yeah, me." I said. "I'm takin' yer dog." I gave the demon-mutt a rub under the chin and unsnapped his chain. The dog licked me real friendly-like.

"No!" Boss yelled. He was so worked up that I thought he musta figgered I was gonna let that demon-mutt at him, which I probly shoulda, but it turned out that he was just worried about losin' his damn dog. Here he was with blood gushin' out of where the right side of his face used to be, and he was cryin' about losin' a dog he'd probably never said a kind word to. "You can't take Duke from me!" he whined, like the dog had just been sucklin' at his teat or somethin.'

"His name ain't Duke," I said, lookin' over the dog. I could see one of his eyes was all messed up, probably from gettin' chaw juice spat in it. Poor dog was scarred and half-blind for life. I said, "His name is Skoal now."

For some reason that made Boss real mad. He started to say, "Listen to me, kid...."

But something in my eyes must have scared him pretty good, cuz he never got past the word *kid*. "Name's Diesel," I said, lightin' a cigarette. "Now why don't you go get yer face put back on?"

Skoal and me got in my truck and took off, and we've been together ever since. We don't talk much, but the two of us have a bond – the kind of bond that only two mean-ass animals can have.

www.ingramcontent.com/pod-product-compliance
Lightning Source LLC
Chambersburg PA
CBHW020002050426
42450CB00005B/286